OVERCOMING Faith

OVERCOMING *Faith*

Dr. Abiola Idowu

OVERCOMING FAITH

This book is written to provide information and motivation to readers. Its purpose is not to render any type of psychological, legal, or professional advice of any kind. The content is the sole opinion and expression of the author, and not necessarily that of the publisher.

Copyright © 2019 by Dr. Abiola Idowu

All rights reserved. No part of this book may be reproduced, transmitted, or distributed in any form by any means, including, but not limited to, recording, photocopying, or taking screenshots of parts of the book, without prior written permission from the author or the publisher. Brief quotations for noncommercial purposes, such as book reviews, permitted by Fair Use of the U.S. Copyright Law, are allowed without written permissions, as long as such quotations do not cause damage to the book's commercial value. For permissions, write to the publisher, whose address is stated below.

Printed in the United States of America.

ISBN   978-1-949746-73-0   (Paperback)
ISBN   978-1-949746-74-7   (Digital)

Lettra Press books may be ordered through booksellers or by contacting:

Lettra Press LLC
18229 E 52nd Ave.
Denver City, CO 80249
1 303 586 1431 | info@lettrapress.com
www.lettrapress.com

CONTENTS

Preface vii

Chapter 1:	Living By Faith 1
Chapter 2:	Faith That Works 12
Chapter 3:	Have Faith in Your Potential 23
Chapter 4:	Victory Over Death (No Premature death) 32
Chapter 5:	You Can Stay Healthy 36
Chapter 6:	Sound Health 49
Chapter 7:	Why God Heals 59
Chapter 8:	Reigning King 65
Chapter 9:	Why Praise? (Part 1) 73
Chapter 10:	Why Praise (Part 2) 82
Chapter 11:	Why Praise? (Part 3) 87
Chapter 12:	The Connecting Force (Part 1) 90
Chapter 13:	The Connecting Force (Part 2) 100

PREFACE

Everything you need is provided by God in the realm of the spirit. The challenge is that you cannot see into the spirit realm. Faith is the vehicle that takes you into the realm of the spirit. Because everything physical has a spiritual root, you need faith to access the realm of the spirit, where all things God has prepared for you is released into your hand. Many believers do not know this, and, as a result, they struggle in life to get that which is already done.

The finished work of our Lord Jesus Christ is a work of complete restoration to bring you to an Edenic experience. 2 Peter 1:3 says, "according as his divine power hath given unto us all things that *pertain* unto life and godliness…," but all these things come through the "knowledge of him that has called us to glory and virtue." Everything you need is provided, but to get the provision, it is necessary to know it, understand it, lay hold of it by faith, and then begin to enjoy your blessing. Through this book, God will open your eyes and you will learn how to release your faith to receive everything that belongs to you.

In studying Overcoming Faith, you will come to understand: 1) the word of God contains the description of what is already in the store house for every believer to lay hold on by faith; 2) the covenant between God and Jesus, which by grace makes all the promises of God yours; 3) how to release your faith to all that is yours; 4) what faith is and what faith is not; 5) how to discover your covenant rights with God and make them work for you; 6) how you can walk in health, and live long to fulfill God's plan for your life; 7) how and why God heals; 8) why praise remains the most potent force in the world for victory and conquest; 9) how your translation into the kingdom of God has ended your toiling and struggling on earth; 10) how to walk in your inheritance and live a constant life of joy, peace and blessing; and much more. As you study Overcoming Faith, God of heaven will turn your destiny around to the glory of His name, in the mighty name of Jesus Christ.

By the grace of God, I decided to write this book because I discovered that faith is misunderstood so much that many are confused and fearful, believing they don't have enough faith to affect Divine intervention in their life challenges. It is lack of understanding that makes faith difficult to grasp. As I pondered why a child of God, whom Jesus Christ died for, would live a life totally devoid of the evidence and effect of redemption, the Lord steered my spirit to write this book so that children of God can experience heaven on earth.

CHAPTER 1

Living By Faith

One reason faith is not working in the lives of many people is because faith is not taught. Most people think they are operating their faith, when what they are really doing is operating in mental assent. What is mental assent? Mental assent is a subtle form of self-deception. With mental assent, you believe something in your head and you agree, approve, and confirm that it is right and righteous. The problem is that you believe it in your head, but not in your heart. This is faith without action.

For example, let's see how people look at the Word. They believe it is true because it is written in the Bible, but when it comes to applying the Word to their lives, it becomes a problem. And faith makes life fake if you can't apply the Word or the faith that you think you have to your life.

Read this chapter carefully as we go into the practicality of living by faith. Faith is not difficult, it just seem difficult because it is not taught.

By redemption everything is restored to us in Christ. The moment you are born again, the finished work of Jesus Christ bestows on you everything that He died for; that means that everything Jesus enjoys, you can enjoy. The same privileges that are open to everyone in Heaven is available to you right now.

Healing belongs to us. We are not looking for healing. It's our right. He said, "By His stripes we are healed." In other words, the price needed to bring healing to every one of us is already paid.

Not that He will pay for it; He has already paid for it. Many will say, "I want God to heal me." Jesus Christ is not going to heal you. He has already healed you.

But I can hear you asking the question, "If that is true, then why am I not healed?" It's because you don't believe. You asked God to heal the pain in your leg, but you still feel symptoms of the pain. The enemy will tell you that God didn't heal you because you are still feeling the pain. But you must believe that God has already healed you and now you are waiting on the manifestation of that healing.

We don't need to begin to think about salvation. Salvation already belongs to us because we are saved by grace through faith. Prosperity already belongs to us. God didn't put a bunch of powerless people in the church. Power belongs to us. Strength belongs to us. Dominion belongs to us. In fact, we don't have to pay any price to get it, because it is already ours.

The point is, we obtain all this by faith. In Mark 11:24, the Bible says, "Therefore I say to you, whatever things you ask when you pray, believe that you receive them, and you will have them." In other words, if you have a desire, you can receive any desire, if you believe. If you believe what the Bible says, you will see the glory of God.

The Bible tells me in Mark 9:23, "All things are possible to him that believes." When you see scriptures like this, you begin to question yourself, "Is it true? Does it really mean we can have whatsoever we desire?" The Bible says God is not a man that He should lie. So yes, it is true. That scripture is an open check to anyone. You must believe. If you get nothing else out of this chapter, get that "you must believe." God says you can have anything you desire—money, progress, breakthrough, health, fulfillment in every area of your life. The key is the Bible says it to us.

John 3:16 tells us "For God so loved the world." The same person that said that said "Except a man is born again, he cannot see the Kingdom Of God." Now do you believe you are born again? The same God said it. I think that is where the problem is. We don't know what to believe. And many believe nothing, but still claim they are operating in faith.

Make no mistake about it—the death and resurrection of Jesus put everything in Heaven and on Earth under the authority of Jesus. Redemption covers the past, present and the future. In fact, because He died and rose from the dead, no other person, force or forces, no other being, has the key to his hand except Jesus. He's the one that determines what happens here. Not even the Almighty God. The Bible says God has given to Him everything. He declared himself in Revelation 1:18, "I am He who lives, and was dead, and behold, I am alive forever more. Amen. And I have the keys of Hades and of Death." In other words, you can't even die without His approval.

The word hell is different from death. I believe hell is a place of no return. Nobody in Christ Jesus is permitted to be locked up for life. No matter how bad your situation is, there is hope. Why? Because that situation never held the key. Redemption gave the key back to Jesus.

Jesus was talking to his disciples in Matthew 28:18. "And Jesus came and spoke to them, saying, 'All authority has been given to me in heaven and on earth.'" In other words, Jesus determines what happens here. Everything that He died for is put together in a document called a testament. If you want to enjoy your life, go to the testament and find out what Jesus Christ paid for on your behalf.

Let's look at this from another viewpoint. If your dad or granddad is dead and he had a lot of property and money, he probably left a will, or a testament. The will (testament) will be interpreted by an attorney. If the attorney misinterprets the will, your dad or granddad is not there to say, "No, that is not what I meant."

But in Jesus' case, He is not dead. He is alive, and He can challenge what is written if what you are supposed to have is not given to you. Go to the document called the testament and you can get what belongs to you and apply it to your situation. The moment you apply it to your situation, it is taking the step of faith. The testament rules over everything, and the testament is so powerful that it cannot fail because somebody went for it.

There is an agreement between the God of the universe that as long as He is on the throne, the testament stands. The Bible tells us in Matthew 24:35 that you have a future. Not only do you have a future, you also have a present. The testament shows you who you are and what belongs to you as a member of Jesus' body. And because it is legally yours, you can never be denied it.

But if you don't know that it's yours, the enemy will play on your intelligence and cheat you. And that is exactly what is happening in the body of Christ today. We are crying to God to help us to get what is already ours.

In Genesis 17:7-8, God made an agreement with Abraham. God said, "I will establish my covenant between me and thee, and thy seed after thee in their generations for an everlasting covenant, to be a God unto thee, and to thy seed after thee." The covenant goes beyond Abraham, to the seed that came after him. "And I will give unto thee, and to thy seed after thee, the land wherein thou art a stranger, all the land of Canaan, for an everlasting possession; and I will be their God." God said that, it was documented, and it became a testament. We should not be crying about anything. We should be dancing and praising God because it is already done.

The problem is this: these things are not what our senses can understand. It is not in the realm of the physical, it is in the realm of faith. When the testament is released, there is nothing in the physical that can justify that what God said is true. In fact, everything will be speaking and standing against that word as if God lied. If you want to check or verify the testament in the physical, you will mess up big time, because there is nothing in the sense.

Hebrews 11:1: Now faith is the assurance (title deed, confirmation) of things hoped for (divinely guaranteed), and the evidence of things not seen {the conviction of their reality.) Faith comprehends as fact what cannot be experienced by the physical senses. (AMP).

The only evidence that you have is that God has spoken. There is no evidence in the physical sense. If you can see it in the Word, then believe it. If it's in the testament, then believe it. Don't wait to see it with your eyes to believe it. In fact, if what God tells you appears in the physical, it may not be real. It must be in the realm of faith.

Joshua 6:1: Now Jericho {a fortified city with high walls} was tightly closed because {of the people's fear} of the sons of Israel; no one went out or came in.

The children of Israel were going to the Promised Land. Remember what God had told their father, Abraham. He said, "I'm going to be a God to them." He told Abraham, "Your children shall possess the gates of their enemies. God remains faithful. He never lies. Now the children of Israel met an obstacle called the wall of Jericho.

Joshua 6:2: And the LORD said unto Joshua, See, I have given into thine hand Jericho, and the king thereof, and the mighty men of valour

Does that not sound crazy? The city was walled; nobody came in and nobody went out. There was no weapon in the house of Israel, and God told them, "I have given unto you, the city." You can't verify that in the physical sense. And to make it worse, God gave them a suicide mission.

Joshua 6:3: ...and ye shall compass the city, all ye men of war, and go round about the city once, Thus shalt thou do this six days.

They should have been dead by the sixth day, because the people of Jericho knew the children of Israel were there, and they knew that the children of Israel were their enemy. That is why they tightened their security. Now, how do you watch your enemies walk around your city for six days and do nothing?

The reason the things you have been believing God for have not yet come is because you are looking for evidence. You can't believe God said it because there is no proof that it's going to come to pass. The more you think you believe God, the more it looks as if God lied. God didn't lie.

How did the Israelites get into a city that is walled? They marched around the city for six days. The people of Jericho had trained men of war with prepared battle outfits. How can they simply stand idly by and do nothing as the children of Israel marched around the city.

Joshua 6:4: And seven priests shall bear before the ark seven trumpets of ram's horns, and the seventh day shall compass the city seven times. And the priest shall blow the trumpets.

The Israelites were not being quiet. They were announcing to the people of Jericho, "We are here to kill you."

That was how the One who made the heaven and the earth designed victory for His children. Because He told Abraham a long time ago, "It's already in the testament that if you face any obstacle, I will be your God." Many times we raise our challenges of life above the One who made a covenant with us. We talk about the challenges instead of talking about the greatness of our God. Your faith can't work until you are standing on what the testament says, not what your feelings are saying. Not your theory, not your scan results, not your bank account, not your friend's view, not your family background. You stand upon what the testament says.

You can trust God by what He said and not trust the report that your senses are giving you. In Romans 8:8, the Bible says, "Flesh can never please God." They that are in the flesh cannot please God. It's not possible. God says He's my healer when my back is in pain. Now there is evidence in your body of pain, but there are evidences in the word of God that by His stripes you are healed.

When I came to an understanding of John 15:5, I said to myself, "Wake up. You are fruitful. You are wonderful. Look at the beauty of the flowers. See generations eating of the food of your life." I saw it. I am the true vine, ye are the branches. It is the branches that bring the flower. You can't see the beauty of the flowers and pretend it does not exist. That is why I experience favor every day. I draw life from God. Why? The branch cannot survive without the stem, and the same source that strengthens the stem, strengthens the branch. He said my leaves shall not whither and whatsoever I do shall prosper.

I don't think about failure. I really don't. Because if I start failing, that means I am cut off from the vine. The Bible said, "Even if they cut you down, you will sprout again." Don't let the challenges of life make you depressed. Because you are the true branch of the true vine. Evil will always come around and try to snare you. But those that dwell in the secret place of the Most High shall abide under the shadow of the Almighty.

The Bible talks about a thousand who shall fall. The people that are falling—God created them too. The ten thousand that fell—God created them too. The reason you are not part of those that are falling is because of where you belong. That is why, even if you walk in the valley of the shadow of death, you will fear no evil.

Pay careful attention to this verse because this is what you can apply to your own life. In 2 Kings 7:1-2, the Bible says, "Then Elisha said, 'Hear ye the word of the LORD; Thus saith the LORD, To morrow about this time shall a measure of fine flour be sold for a shekel, and two measures of barley for a shekel, in the gate of Samaria.

² Then a lord on whose hand the king leaned answered the man of God, and said, Behold, if the LORD would make windows in heaven, might this thing be? And he said, Behold, thou shalt see it with thine eyes, but shalt not eat thereof.'"

The minister of finance in Israel at that time was a good man. What killed him was he looked for evidence in the senses. The Word of The Lord came— "By this time tomorrow."

We limit the Holy one of Israel by waiting for Him to follow human protocols to do what He needs to do. God is more than that.

At that time, the famine was so severe, that people were killing their own children for food. It was much more than what America is going thru right now. If you don't have any food and you kill your dog, or someone else's dog, to eat, you could go to jail. A dog is an animal, but if you kill that animal to eat it, they will surely take you to jail. But in that time, they were actually killing human beings and eating them. They were killing their own children, not their pets.

The Testament is what we deal with in the Kingdom, not the evidence in the economy, not the evidence around us, not the evidence in our community. There is no good news anywhere in the world. The only good news is in the Kingdom of God, and the good news is in the Testament.

Galatians 4:28: Now we, brethren, as Isaac was, are the children of promise.

The point now is, "God do you mean what you are saying?" It is not if the economy improves, you improve. It's coming to a time where people are coming to you to ask, "Are we living in the same place?" I pity people that center their life on a paycheck. You can't be great because Babylon is the one already controlling your life.

> Genesis 26:1-5: "And there was a famine in the land, beside the first famine that was in the days of Abraham. And Isaac went unto Abimelech king of the Philistines unto Gerar.
>
> ² And the LORD appeared unto him, and said, Go not down into Egypt; dwell in the land which I shall tell thee of:
>
> ³ Sojourn in this land, and I will be with thee, and will bless thee; for unto thee, and unto thy seed, I will give all these countries, and I will perform the oath which I sware unto Abraham thy father;
>
> ⁴ And I will make thy seed to multiply as the stars of heaven, and will give unto thy seed all these countries; and in thy seed shall all the nations of the earth be blessed;
>
> ⁵ Because that Abraham obeyed my voice, and kept my charge, my commandments, my statutes, and my laws."

Remember as Isaac was, so are we brethren.

Put your name everywhere you see "Isaac." God did not say to Isaac "because you are a good man." "You did everything I asked you to do, I will bless you." No. He said, "Because of the covenant I made with your Dad, I will do all these things unto you and your seed." When God spoke to him, there was nothing physical to justify that he was going to be blessed. In fact, the Word of the Lord explains that the Philistines envied him; they stopped everything he wanted to do. "But God, you told me I'm going to be great. Why is it that any breakthrough has stopped? The first one didn't work, the second one didn't work, and the third one didn't work." If it were you and I, we would have thought, "I don't think God meant what He said. Maybe He's not even God."

God is taking you to a place that, when your breakthrough comes, no one is going to be able to stop it. God promised that it is going to be okay. But you could be thinking, "This is the seventh month, and I don't see anything. Maybe it's because of my sin." It's not your sin. It's because God is coming so big that the people who are trying to stop your breakthrough are coming to serve you. See what happened to the people that envied Isaac.

I read that scripture like this: So Biola sowed in that land, and received in the year 2013 one-hundred-fold, and the Lord blessed me.

Verse 13: ...and the man waxed great, and went forward, and grew until he became very great.

In the time of famine, somebody was greater than the people he met in their land. That's faith. You must put yourself in that place with Isaac. Meditate on it until you think you are going out to your Bentley or Mercedes. Walk out of those shackles, walk out of that oppression, and walk out of that sickness. Now, whatsoever they tell you, it's not true until you agree.

Verse 14: ...for he had possession of flocks, and possession of herds and great store of servants; and the Philistines envied him.

That is exactly where God is taking you. You are going forward, you are breaking bounds. Famine can't stop you. The enemy can't delay your speed. This is your season of greatness; this is your time of speed. By the authority in the name of Jesus, people will envy your success. Receive it in the Name of Jesus. Say, my faith is working.

There is a glory ahead that supersedes this present gloominess. It's already in the Testament. Go search it. The Testament is a surety of our destiny. It never fails. The redemption of Jesus gave to us the totality of everything. Everything is inclusive. Not only what we lost in the garden, but things to prevent us from losing it again. The beauty of redemption is even when you are the lowest of the low, the power of Jesus can take you to the top without the influence of anyone. That's the beauty of it. We are not begging God to save us, it's already paid for. We are not begging God to heal us, we are already healed. We are not begging God to give us money. Money is already a part of our redemption.

Ephesians 1:3: Blessed be the God and Father of our Lord Jesus Christ, who hath blessed us with all spiritual blessings in heavenly places in Christ.

The moment you come to Christ, everything is in your account. Faith sees that because God has given it to you, and I evidence it in the Testament. You begin to draw from it and declare it, because you know that the God that promises never lies. What you are experiencing in the physical realm no longer disturbs your mind because you are concentrating on what He said about you in the Word. You don't beg for a gift. It is called a gift because it is at the discretion of the person giving it to you whether you are qualified for it or not. You are not the one that decides if you qualify for the gift. The person giving you the gift feels this is what you are worth. God gave you everything you will ever need as a gift because Jesus Christ told him you are qualified. Your faith in the fact that He died and rose from the dead was the qualification needed to be counted worthy of the gift.

The greatest force in the universe is the power of the Holy Spirit. The Holy Spirit is given to you—it's inside of you whether you know it or not. You can't talk about weakness or tiredness in the face of Acts 1:8: But ye shall receive power, after that the Holy Ghost is come upon you; and ye shall be witnesses unto me both in Jerusalem and in all of Judaea, and in Samaria, and unto the uttermost part of the earth.

The word power means ability. You receive ability when the Holy Ghost comes upon you. The Bible says it is the Holy Spirit that convinces you that Jesus Christ died and rose from the dead. If the Holy Spirit is inside of you right now, and you know God is not lying, why say, "I don't know, I don't feel?" That is why you are still in the sense realm.

> How do I know I have the Holy Spirit? Because I feel like falling? No. I know I have the Holy Spirit because the Word of God says it. John 14:15-16 says, "If ye love me, keep my commandments.

> And I will pray the Father, and he shall give you another Comforter, that he may abide with you for ever;"

Whether you are down or up, the Holy Spirit is in you. You may ask, "How do I activate the Holy Spirit?" Begin to say it to yourself. "I have the Holy Spirit, and the same spirit inside of Jesus is in me. Greater is He that is in me than he that is in the world." Then look at the challenges face to face. If the challenges can't win over Jesus, then the challenges can't win over you. Because God is not a man that He should lie. The same thing He packaged inside of Jesus, He packaged inside of you.

The Word of God is the gas for your life. Look in the scripture and find out what the Bible says about you. I have shown you. Now you must go and search it for yourself. There is no Pastor that reads the Bible for church members.

Say this with me, "My faith is working. I am going forward. I am blessed, I am lifted. The favor of God is upon my life. I am redeemed, all is well with me." Shout "Hallelujah."

Can you see greatness now? The Bible says as Isaac was, so are you. I'd like you to begin to declare into your life right now. You have seen what the Bible says concerning your life. It is already in the Testament. The Bible says as many of us that believe, we have passed dead to life. It's yours and my responsibility to believe. When God speaks, use your tongue to empower it. How many has had the privilege of being in the court of law when a will is being read? The inheritance of your life is in the book, but until you say it with your mouth, it is still in the letters. My faith is working. I am blessed. I am going forward. As Isaac was, so I am. In the mighty name of Jesus, no disease, no affliction will survive in my body, because He took my infirmities, by His stripes I am healed. He was made poor, so that through His poverty, I might be rich. I am rich! My faith is working.

CHAPTER 2

Faith That Works

As you read through this book, God will begin to change your life and give you a befitting destiny in the mighty name of Jesus. Until you understand the ways of God, it will be difficult to see the act of God. The Bible says that the Lord revealed his ways unto Moses and his acts to the children of Israel. It is the ways of God that will bring you waves on the earth. God has not changed. He's still delivering, He's still healing and He's still blessing His people. God's ways are His principles, and His principles are the keys to His blessings. There is no situation that God cannot handle if we have an understanding of His ways.

Hosea 12:13 gives a clear word from heaven. There the Bible says Israel was delivered by a prophet, and by a prophet he was preserved. That means that the destiny of God's people was handed over to the prophet He sent. Anything can happen in the life of anyone who believes in the Word of the Lord.

The Bible says Israel was in trouble and turmoil and it looked as if the situation was not going to change. The enemy was crying against their destiny and their inheritance. 2 Chronicles 20:20: "Believe in the Lord your God, so shall ye be established; believe his prophets, so shall ye prosper." In other words, God handed over the prosperity, the peace and the healing of His people into the hands of His prophet.

When Jesus Christ came to earth, He said, I do nothing by myself; He said the words that I speak unto you are not my words.

He said, it is the Father that works in me that doeth the work. I just hear Him, and speak what He said. God is committed to the fulfillment of those words through all humility.

Jesus sent me, a prophet, to declare the Word of the Lord for humanity. God sent me to the city of Jacksonville, FL, to tell the devil enough is enough, and it's time for God's people to enter into their inheritance. This is going to happen whether the devil likes it or not. We have an assignment in the world—to snatch God's people from the hand of the wicked one, by the Word of the Lord.

In Luke chapter ten, starting in verse 17, the Bible says, "The seventy returned again with joy. They did not come with reproach, they returned with joy saying Lord; even the devils are subject unto us by Thy name." Among the seventy were Thomas the doubter, and Judas Iscariot, the one that betrayed Jesus. Because there was an assignment in their hand, the Bible says they returned with joy and in verse 18, "He said unto them, I beheld Satan as lightning fell from heaven," because somebody sent them.

The One that sent them handled the enemy that stood against them. It wasn't because they were eloquent in the way they spoke; it wasn't because they spoke better than others. It's because someone sent them and the One that sent them was the One doing the work.

God sent me too, and this time cancer has to hear, diabetes has to hear, multiple sclerosis has to hear, HIV has to hear, oppression of darkness has to hear, poverty has to hear and bow in the mighty name of Jesus. The season of submission of all forces to the name of Jesus has finally come. I cannot wait to see the people of God delivered. I have seen God deliver; I've seen God heal. With God all things are possible. God can turn things around.

Some years ago, a lady came to my house. When I answered the door, she asked to speak to my dad. She came looking for the man of God that everyone was talking about. But when she saw me, I understood that she was not expecting to see someone of my stature and so young in age. She expected an old man with gray hair. We were both just looking at one another, and she finally said, "Can you please go and call your dad for me?" At that same time, a church member came to the house and greeted me, saying, "Oh,

Man of God." The woman who had come for prayer realized I was the one she was looking for. She was so surprised.

As we began to talk, I realized she had elephantiasis. As she was talking to me, I was looking at her legs, and suddenly the anointing of the Holy Spirit came upon me. The Lord said to me that I should give her the flip flops that I was wearing. I took them off and gave them to her and told her to put them on. The scripture tells us that the anointing that is upon the Priest, flows through the beards and goes into his skirts. That means that whatsoever the anointed touches is anointed. The woman put on my flip flops and instantly her leg deflated. The Lord touched the leg and the leg was healed. The woman screamed at the top of her lungs. I was as surprised as she was, because I had no idea what The Lord would do when He told me to have her put on my flip flops. Everyone in the house came running to see what was happening. And let me tell you, that was the healing, because the power in the name of Jesus can subdue every force of darkness. Amen.

God is not glorified in your afflictions. He is only glorified in your blessing. Each time Jesus performs a miracle, God is glorified. People glorified God and they said we have never seen it in this version. God wants to glorify Himself again in the world today, and we are coming with the force of heaven to put into silence all the works of the enemy in your life through the power of the Holy Spirit, in the mighty name of Jesus Christ. I'd like you to set your heart in place. When God was about to rescue humanity, He sent a man named Noah and He asked Noah to build an ark. But when the flood came, the people that entered the ark were saved. They got their deliverance. God worked.

How do you know a prophet? Because what he says comes to past. It's time to see God do in your city what He has done in other parts of the world. Because God said enough to that sickness, enough to that affliction, enough to that problem that looks as if it is bigger than your faith, bigger than your God. There is nothing that can stand against you, because the Lord that made the heaven and the earth has remembered you, and is ready to rescue you from the hand of the wicked one. "And the seventy returned again with joy." You are returning this time with great joy, with great satisfaction, with great rejoicing, with great testimonies in the name of Jesus.

It does not take one-hundred years for God to rewrite people's testimonies. Whether you have a history that you received from your parents, whether you have a curse over your life, whether the enemy has told you stories that are not true, whether you have even spoken to yourself because of the experiences you have had or the experiences of others, I have good news for you. Just as the ark of Noah rescued that generation, the ark of Jesus is here through His servant to rescue you.

When the Lord told me to come to Jacksonville and start His ministry, I did not even know how to pronounce "Jacksonville." I used to call it "Jacksonvilly." I didn't know that Jacksonville was a city in Florida. I was in Nigeria, and the Lord told me that I was to come to America and start His work here. I heard the Lord clearly give me the mission statement for His Church: "Raise unto me soldiers that will walk on the surface of the earth like Christ. Release men and women to their destiny."

It's time to take the earth for the King, and the King is already here. His name is Jesus, the Son of the Living God, and He has sent me to declare that council to humanity, and because He is the one that said it, He is the one that is going to back it up. Even as you are reading this book, I'd like you to raise your right hand and connect with faith as I pray this prayer of healing and deliverance, breakthrough and joy into your life. And my Father that dwells in me, will do the work.

Father, Lord, I stand upon the word of the Lord this day, and I declare by the anointing of the Holy Spirit, whatsoever is holding these people bound—either in their lives, either in their homes, their joys, their academics—I break that force in the mighty name of Jesus Christ. The word of the Lord tells me that at the name of Jesus every knee shall bow, all things in heaven, things on earth, things under the earth, and every tongue must confess that Jesus is Lord. I declare right now, by the power that raised Jesus Christ from the dead, the forces of darkness are broken in your life! The power of evil is broken in your life. The power of stagnation is broken in your life. That place that you have been applying to for that job, they will call you this time, in the name of Jesus Christ. Enter into that which belongs to you. Your inheritance is released right now. Your joy is released right now. Your peace is released right now. Your health is released right now. I speak miracles into your life. I release signs and wonders upon your life. Receive it in Jesus mighty name. It is well with you. Thank you, Father, in Jesus name. Amen.

Now if you don't know that God is a jealous God, you don't know his character. Many people serve God, but they don't know the character of the God they serve. And because of that, many times the enemy gives them the wrong image of The Almighty God. That is why a lot of people, when they go through a lot of situations on earth or in their lives, they think that God brought them to it. No. God may use that situation to glorify His name, but He does not bring people into their problems. Each time God sees you in a problem, He is angry about that problem, that situation. We saw in Exodus 20:5 that God told the children of Israel when He was giving them the Law, "He said to Moses, thou shall not bow down thyself to them, nor serve them, for I the Lord thy God am a jealous God visiting the iniquities of the fathers upon the children unto the third and fourth generation of them that hate me." In other words, God cannot stand anything taking His place in our Life. When people are going thru situations, those situations want to be God in their lives. Sickness wants to be a god. It takes all your attention. Poverty wants to be a god. Affliction, joblessness, drug addiction wants to be a god in your life. Each time those things takes their place, they don't allow you to serve God the way you want to.

In John 1:12, God said as many that receive Him, as many that trust in His name, to them He gave the power to become sons of God. And if you hold God's sons bound, if you hold God's daughters bound, you are going to face the wrath of their Father. When you have an understanding that Pharaoh represents limitations, he represents bondage, failure, slavery, poverty, he represents anything that stand against freedom. And God said go and tell that situation, "You can't hold my son, you can't hold my daughter. If you try it, I'll kill you." That's what God is saying. Because God is a jealous God. And if God said it to Israel who was not under the new covenant, how much more is God going to fight for His children, who Jesus Christ died for?

There is a challenge in the church of Jesus today. We are yet to understand that we are in the world, but not of the world. And the system of this world is not meant for us. We are far above that. We are not living under their government, under their system. Government is Jesus the Son of the living God. No wonder the Bible says, in Isaiah 9:6 "for unto us a child is born and unto us a son is given and the government shall be upon his shoulder."

The government of God is right here on the earth, to let the people see freedom, to let people see liberty thru his Son Jesus Christ that came and died for our sin. We are bought with a price, and it's time for that price to begin to speak—no more servitude and no more slavery. We are born to be fruitful, we are born to multiply, we are born to replenish, subdue, and dominate the earth in the mighty name of Jesus Christ. The Bible says, "When the wicked beareth rule, people mourn." But when the righteous is in government, the Bible says the people rejoice. You need to know that the government of this world has become the government of God and Christ, and He shall reign forever.

Once you are born again, God gives you the measure of faith. Romans 12:3: "For I say, through the grace given unto me, to every man that is among you, not to think of himself more highly than he ought to think; but to think soberly, according as God hath dealt to every man the measure of faith." The faith that He is referring to is the God kind of faith.

The Bible says that all men have not faith. This means they have natural faith, but not the God kind of faith. Natural faith is based on senses. It's based on seeing something and being convinced—your senses are convinced that it is so. For example, the chair that you are sitting on. You have faith that the chair you are sitting in right now will hold your weight. If you doubted it, you would not have sat down. Am I right? That is natural faith.

The faith I'm talking about is the faith that comes from the Word of God. And for the most part it does not agree with our senses. Sense knowledge is not faith because you can reason it out. But faith knowledge makes no sense. Our mind has been trained by a system that is based on our senses, our satisfaction, and our reasoning. You have reasoned it out with input from the five senses.

Let's look at the definition of faith:

Hebrew 11:1: Now faith is the substance of things hoped for, the evidence of things not seen.

In other words, not perceived by the senses.

What is your evidence? It's faith.

Let's look at that same scripture in the amplified version:

Hebrews 11:1: Now faith is the assurance (title deed, confirmation) of things hoped for (divinely guaranteed), and the evidence of things not seen {the conviction of their reality—faith comprehends as fact what cannot be experienced by the physical senses}.

In order for you to truly operate in faith, you must leave your senses behind.

I know that I am saying some things that are hard for you to digest, but before you can have overcoming faith, you must understand faith. What stymies the average person is having to believe something for which you have no natural proof to the point that you are willing to give your all for what you believe.

If I encounter one-hundred people today and ask them if they have faith in God, I can guarantee you that ninety-percent of them will say yes. But if we took the time to dissect their faith, the majority of that ninety-percent have misplaced faith. Misplaced faith is the act of trying to have faith in something else a little bit other than God.

But faith demands that God not only be your source, but your only source. People will ask, "How can I have faith in someone that is invisible?" We know that John 6 tells us that God is a Spirit. And spirits can't be seen. That's why we must meditate on the definition of faith. Read John 6 and let it resonate in your spirit. Once you are clear on the definition of faith, it will be much easier to achieve it.

You must be mindful of things that hinder your faith.

There is another spirit that when it operates, it can hinder your faith. That spirit is fear.

Yes, fear is a spirit too. (2 Timothy 1:7)

That's why you can't deal with fear naturally. You can't deal with any spirits naturally.

People will believe ignorant stuff. But when you tell them that God will do something for them, they have a problem with that.

Fear cannot be dealt with naturally. We see that in Deuteronomy 7:1, "When the Lord shall bring thee into the land whither thou goest to possess it, and hath cast out many nations before thee, the Hibites, and the Jebusites, seven nations greater and mightier than thou." Moses was directing the people to take them into the promise land. These are types of spirits and strongmen.

They are stronger than you are. If you are born again, you are not without God. God is in you, and greater is He that is in you than he that is in the world.

And when your faith is operating in that way, you can cast any spirit out there.

The spirit of fear didn't come when the person got frightened. The spirit of fear was already there. Being frightened is when it manifested. It was there all the time, waiting for an opportunity.

When you go into the Promise land is when the spirit rises up.

You are going to get hurt; you are going to fail; people are going to laugh at you and talk about you. Let's face reality—you don't have enough money to dream that way. Let's be reasonable…

Fear makes you back up but there is a promise land on the other side of your fear.

What does it take to get through it? Faith.

And God has given every one of us that are born again a measure of faith.

But it is up to you to develop your faith. It is faith that does the work. Faith is the servant of the believer.

It's important that you know what kind of faith we are talking about. We are talking about God kind of faith, not about human faith because human faith can't do anything for you;

But the God kind of faith can move a mountain. The God kind of faith can take care of any impossible situation.

The more developed you are in fear, the faster the fear will manifest.

The more developed your faith is, the faster it will manifest.

The Lord has reminded me of one of my daughters in the Lord. She had a great fear of spiders. If a spider was in her house, she could not sleep in that house that night. She began to hear the Word and the message on fear, and she discovered through the Word that fear was a spirit and it did not come from God. From that moment, she decided she was not going to let the fear of spiders rule her anymore. And, of course, the enemy let her see a spider in her car while she was driving. When she saw the spider, she began to cast down the spirit of fear. When stopped at a red-light, she took her shoe and hit the spider so hard that it died right there. This was a big deal for her, because in the past she would have surely had an accident after seeing a spider in the car with her. Praise the Lord.

Faith is the substance of things hoped for. We must get out of fear.

Every time Jesus showed up, He said fear not. When the angel showed up, he said fear not. Why? Because fear can't receive from God. Fear won't let you receive your promises. Fear is a huge hindrance to your faith.

Cast down the fear. And walk by faith.

How does faith come? By hearing. By hearing what? The word of God. You need to feed your faith. Feed it every morning, feed it in your car, feed it at home. Don't let the enemy get comfortable in your home, because he brings fear, and destruction.

Faith is a living thing. It's a servant. It's a power.

Sometimes we need to sit down and meditate on our faith, examine our faith, talk about our faith.

What is faith? How does it work?

Nothing can withstand faith. Whenever you start hearing the word of faith, the enemy tries to attack because the enemy does not want your faith to grow. Faith comes out of your heart. It's time for us to use some faith. It's time to let our faith work for us.

Faith is an instrument

You use faith like a surgeon uses a scalpel

Luke 17:5: ...and the apostles said unto the Lord, increase our faith.

People want to have better faith by the laying on of hands. But that's not how it works. You must do something. You must act on faith.

Do you increase your muscles by sitting home eating apple pie, and saying praise God, I receive some more muscles? No, you go to the gym and work out.

The more you use your faith the more it will increase.

The principle of how you use faith is that you take faith first, as a seed and say it. Once you say it, you sow it. Where do you sow it? In your heart. Your heart is designed to bring forth whatever is sown in it.

Don't expect this to happen overnight. It takes development.

It takes time; it takes patience.

But it will bring forth. No matter what picture the enemy shows you, you must exercise your faith. The enemy will always try to distract you.

Faith takes us above the natural world. And once you get into faith, your destiny cannot be denied. Faith now is as a servant

Faith does the work for you. It is like tennis. Let the racket do the work. Let your faith do the work. There is power in faith.

Faith has a voice.

Whenever you are whining and complaining, you are not in Faith. That won't get God's attention. As a matter of fact, in the wilderness, whining and complaining kept the Israelites from going into Canaan. The attitude of complaining and criticizing all the time, or whining is an attitude that opens the door for the enemy. Don't always talk about your problems. Don't talk defeat or failure. Keep those words out of your mouth.

Don't listen to religion. Religion tries to reject your God-like communication; it tries to reject righteousness. Many times, we struggle trying to find faith when we first need to concentrate on getting the right image of God, and then faith will come. Religion is designed to reject your God-like identity. Because you have been saved, you are kings and ambassadors.

Acts 17:29 teaches that you are God's offspring. God will let you go as far as your faith will carry you. Don't let the enemy distract you.

Say to yourself, "I am going to look to Jesus. He is the author and finisher of my faith. I want my faith to qualify me. It's time for me to own some of this business."

Let your faith work for you. Faith gives you direct access to God. Faith comes by believing God's Word

You've got to get angry. The enemy has kept you bound with fear, unbelief, and unforgiveness while he stole your stuff. You have to say, "I want my stuff back." The enemy has stolen your stuff and you can't let him have it. You have to take the fight to the enemy. You have to say, "I know who I am, and you can't handle me. And if you do, you still have to deal with my Father." Get bold and say, "Cross this line and I'll knock your head off. Get out of my house. Get away from my kids. Get away from my job and my finances. Get out of my life." Come out of yourself. Stop trying to be proper and composed. Let the enemy know that you mean business. Give God some crazy praise and rejoice in the Lord. The enemy can't stand that.

Don't say, "Well, yeah, I have faith." No. You must work your faith, and then you will have the faith that works.

The gospel of our Lord Jesus Christ is total. It's not just to bring you to church. It's to bring you to a level where you have influence and impact on this earth. You won't see a king or a queen without influence and impact of royalty. The time has come for you to shine, and as I declare the word of the Lord upon your life today, I command your situation to change. I command everything around you to begin to sing the glory of God.

CHAPTER 3

Have Faith in Your Potential

When we talk about potential, we are talking about what God put inside of you that you are yet to use. Potential is unexposed ability. It is the reserved power; it is your untapped strength. It is your capped ability. Unused success. It is what I call a dormant gift. It's there, but it is dormant. Hidden talents. It is what you are capable of doing that you have not yet done. It is where you are capable of going, but you have never yet gone. It is what you are capable of being, that you have never yet been. It is what you can imagine that you have not yet imagined. It is what you can accomplish that you have not yet accomplished. When we talk about potential, we are talking about a deposit of God inside of you that is yet to be maximized. Everyone in the universe has things inside that God put inside of us to bring Glory to His name. That is what is called potential.

Everything has within itself a seed. Everything you see started as a seed. The death of a seed is an abortion of a forest. If I am holding in my hand a common seed, all you see is a seed, but that's a plantation in my hand. If that seed dies as a seed in my hand, I have successfully destroyed a plantation.

The Bible told us that a seed is a foundation for potential in Genesis 1:11: "And God said, let the earth bring forth grass, the earth yielding seed and the fruit trees yielding fruit after its kind. Whose seed is in itself upon the earth, and it was so." That means the manifestation of anything starts with the seed inside. God said,

"Let them bring forth according to the seed that is within them." There are no empty creatures.

Everybody came with something. From the beginning, the design of the Almighty God has been, if I'm going to get this thing big, I have to start with a seed, and the potential inside the seed is the harvest you can see tomorrow.

Everything came with a seed form. You are a seed that God is waiting for to bring a harvest. Each creation possesses the ability to be much more than they appear at some point in time. Every seed is a generation carrier.

There are things that are born within you that God designed that will take you to a higher height and manifest its glory in ways you have never witnessed. You complain that things are not working, but God said, "What of the giant inside?" If you nurture that giant you will be too much to handle. But we neglect our giant and are looking for a dwarf. Most of the things we complain about are because we are yet to discover what we are carrying around. You are more than your size. You are greater than what you think because of the invisible deposit of God inside of you.

At creation God made four things happen. The Bible says He created everything for his pleasure.

1. God planned what to create. It was not an idea from an engineer, or from a physician, or from an economist. He had a plan of exactly what He wanted to create. That is why, when He created man, He didn't put his leg where his head is. He created everything by design. He has a plan without your advice or my advice.

2. He decided on his own the kind of material that He used. You are not going to just come around. How many of you have found that everything that God has created, there has been no improvement? You can't improve on the sun, or the moon, or the stars. You can't improve on you the way He created you. Try it. Put your ears on your neck and let's see what it looks like. You can't improve on what God has already established. He is the one that determined the

kind of material He used for his product. He decided to use water to create fish; He decided to use dust to create man.

3. He spoke to the substance that He used for his stuff. Remember, after God put everything together, He said let there be. He spoke to them. He said let there be light. The Lord commanded the water put themselves together, and let them bring forth fishes according to their kind. He spoke to the material that He used for his product.

4. What He spoke to brought forth their results. That is why I know that your life is a life to be celebrated. God spoke to the water and the water began to bring forth what He decided in his heart. Those materials were pregnant with what God saw and He called it out. God look at man and said, "You are seated with Christ in Heavenly places." Don't try to reason it out. He is calling out what He put there. He said you have the Holy Spirit because that is what He put there. When He says, "Be filled with the Holy Spirit," it is none of your business as to how it will get there. All you need to do is to release your faith.

You saw that plant came from the ground, because the ground was pregnant with plant. Animals came from the ground, because the ground was pregnant with animals. Sun, moon and stars—they all came out of the firmament. Because the firmament was full of sun, moon and stars.

You and I came out of Jesus, because Jesus is full of you and me. When God wanted to get man in the first instance, He spoke to himself. He said, "Come; let us create man in our own image." The original Hebrew text says, "Man Be, and Man was." God put himself in you, so that you can continue what He is doing on the earth.

Genesis 5:1-2: This is the book of the generations of Adam, in the day that God created Man. In the likeness of God made He him, male and female, created He them and blessed them, and called their name Adam, in the day when they were created."

When He put them together, Adam and Eve had the same name. Man and woman were in the same body initially before God separated them. He pulled man out of Himself and He named man Adam, but we left that place.

> Ephesians 3:14-15: For this cause I bow my knees unto the Father of our Lord Jesus Christ, Of whom the whole family in heaven and earth is named.

Now He called them out and He named them Adam. He called us out and He named us Jesus. That shows that we have the same potential inside of us, just as Jesus Christ did. The difference between you and Jesus is that you still carry a body and He doesn't. The enemy is working against that in the life of believers and telling you that you are just human. That is not true. You are not just human. Only your covering is human. The real you is not human. The real you is Jesus. The Bible says the whole family in heaven and earth is named after Christ. You are named after the anointed. And the anointing of God inside of you is to bring glory to God.

Isaiah 43:7 says, "Everything I have created, I have created them for my glory." When we talk about glory, there is no shame in glory; there is no oppression in glory. There is no frustration or poverty in glory. If you allow your experience and your past experience of what people are telling you to determine what God said about you, you are slapping Jesus in the face by believing that He did not do what He said He did.

When we talk about redemption, it is a total displacement from what you used to be to what you are supposed to be. It is a total disconnection from the fallen state of Man. You are more than what you have done, because there is so much inside that has not been used.

In every bird there is a flock. In every cow there is a herd. In every man there is a god. Nobody is empty. That is against eternal purpose. If you can agree that God is an awesome God, and you know God does not make mistakes, then you have to agree with this principle of creation—that there is no one who is empty.

In Matthew 25:14-15, Jesus Christ gave instructions to his disciples about the way man supposed to live. He told the parable about a man who was going on a journey. He called all his servants and he gave them gifts according to their ability. And he gave each of them talents. A talent is worth one-million, eighty dollars. The man knew that if he gave one man ten talents, the amount itself will kill him. He gave some five, because they still had some Moses to carry it. He gave some ten. Now in today's world, people are envious of somebody that was given ten talents, but the one who gave them one talent knows they can't handle more.

You have to change your mindset and let God be your source. He gave everyone gifts and He said, occupy until I come. That means you have something to keep you busy all the days of your life. Occupy is not something that you use for four months or five years. There is no retirement age with what God gave you. Because what He put inside of you is to bring glory to Him, not just you, and the more you bring Glory to Him, the more the glory in your life increases, because the pipe that carries water can never be dry. He can't be using you, touching life through you, changing life through you and you look bankrupt. It is not going to happen.

It's unfortunate that all men are sent to the world with credits but many are living without impact. They carry too much and yet they are living with no impact. Don't let yesterday's success tempt you into thinking that you have utilized all things. If God opened your eyes to see what is laying there dormant, you wouldn't be able to sleep.

The rich fool said, "See what my hand has gotten for me. I got this, I got that. And He said, "Today you will be required that soul that you think you want to feed." And the man died a miserable death.

You are not yet what you are supposed to be. Yesterday's accomplishment is just a part of the game. It's not the end of it. If you see the mystery of creation, you will wake up every day and celebrate yourself. God looked at one man, took an ordinary rib out of his body, and another human being came from it. And the bone He took out of that man's body is one of the tiniest bones in the body. God pulled it out and made a woman out from it.

There are so many beings inside of you that are crying to come out. Your own being may not be a woman. Your own being may be prosperity. Your own being may be wisdom. Or it may be an idea that will change the world. One of the tiniest ribs brought out a woman. I don't know what your femur, your fibula is carrying right now, crying that you should just wake up and allow these things to come out. You sit somewhere backbiting, crying, looking for a pity party. Wake up, this is your season.

Suppose Moses died before seeing the burning bush. Who would have delivered Israel? Maybe Israel would have waited more years in bondage. Supposed David died before he killed Goliath. Who would have ruled Israel? Suppose Noah died before the flood. The whole world would have perished. You don't know what the world would have lost without you. Wake up, wake up. Refuse to sleep a useless sleep. When you come to a place in your life, that you know is true, I don't know what all God wants to do thru me, but I know that it is something, and I'm not going to put sleep into my eyes, until I discover it, and my destiny becomes a rallying point, before my assignment on the earth is over.

You don't just say that until you feel good. You decide every day that you will talk to God for twenty or thirty minutes about this. Spend time to seek his word at least twenty or thirty minutes every day until you locate this.

If wishes were horses everybody would ride. You can't just say, "I just know God is going to do something. I just know God is going to move." Nothing will move. It has to be a determination of planning. Every day when you wake up, seek his face. Thirty minutes, forty minutes. You may lose time.

When you are reading this book, you may say, "I am going to start with 20 hours." That's an indication that you won't do anything . Start with what you can afford, and don't let it be less than fifteen minutes. Two minutes seeking God's face won't take you anywhere. You need a minimum of at least fifteen minutes to seek God's face. You will want to spend time reading the scripture for another fifteen minutes, so that every day at least thirty minutes is set apart to spend time and interactions between you and your Maker.

Nobody ever got to the top without the help of heaven, nobody. Neglecting what will change your story and trying to get to the top on your own is like trying to drive a car without any gas. The car will refuse to move and you will blame BMW. But it has nothing to do with BMW, you just need to put gas in the car. You are born to make history. So, start thinking, what will the world lose without me?

To carry this ability inside and refuse to use it is called irresponsibility. There are so many things that are inside of your life that need to shine. Just as there are some things inside me that you need. So if you are partaking in the gifts that I offer, but you aren't releasing your own gifts, then you are stealing from me. The greatest tragedy that can happen to a person is for that person to die with your things. God created things in such a way that I need you, just as you need me. If you are taking something that God has given to me, and you don't release yours, you are starving me. There are so many things inside you. Inventions, investments, songs, books, etc. You just put your gifts on the shelf and you never touch them. You say, "One day something will happen." Nothing will happen one day. Wake up.

Who are You?

This will help you appreciate the stuff you are made of so that whoever comes around you does not hold any strength against you. Who you are is tied directly to where you came from. Your origin. If you don't know your origin, you can't know your identity. God will look at a messed-up life and see a Messiah inside.

People will say bad things about you. They have a right to their opinion but it should not move you. You don't need to defend those things. King James bible calls it "an expected end." The Bible tells us in John 14:6 that nobody can come unto the Son, except the Father who called him. The Son of God said "everyone that the Father has given unto me except the Son or Child of Perdition." When Jesus came, He preached , "Repent, for the Kingdom of God is here." Repent is not a religious word, it is a kingdom word.

If you don't know who you are, the devil will tell you who you are not. Mark 4:15: "And these are they by the way side, where the word is sown; but when they have heard, Satan cometh immediately, and taketh away the word that was sown in their hearts." The enemy comes to steal the word. The enemy will try everything to make sure you don't have a connection to who you are. God looked at Adam and saw the word. He looked at Abraham and He saw a Nation. He sees in the Dark the way you see in the light. Abraham trained his mind to see the way God sees. Remember David. God saw in him a king. And everything God sees comes to past.

In 2 Corinthians, The Bible tells us that the mirror of our life is the scripture. Mirrors are just a reflection of you. God is your source. The word "Father" is from the Hebrew word pater, meaning a source, and sustainer and a provider. Because God is your source, you are made up of God's particles, not dust. Adam lived hundreds of years after he fell, but he was dead, he was eternally separated from God. If God is your source, be in the environment that will help you survive a trial. As long as Adam was in the Garden of Eden, nothing could challenge his Authority. The presence of the Lord will make you who you are. Without His presence, stunted growth occurs.

Another word for hurt is to be stagnant. Something I have discovered about a manufacturer is that if you use their product properly, it will bring glory to the manufacturer. The man who invented electricity did not invent electric shock. Electric shock occurred because of misuse of electricity. If you ever bought a new product, the moment you open the box you see the owner's manual. On the first page, it says in bold letters, "Read this manual entirely before you use this product." Ninety-nine percent of the people don't read the manual.

The reason destiny is blank is because when God sent you, He told you to read the manual, the Bible. If you compare yourself to others, you will wound yourself and destroy those plans. The Bible says, "They who compare themselves are not wise."

If you are not experiencing joy and peace in your life, return yourself to your Manufacturer so that He can fix you. Say, "Father, you are my source and my strength. Fix me." He will always pronounce over your life, not what you feel, but what He designed you for.

The Bible says it's a mystery. Christ is in you. Begin to see who you are. You are the body of Christ. He's in Heaven, and you are on Earth but He lives in you. You live in Heaven right now as if you are the one there.

> Hebrews 9:24: "For Christ is not entered into the holy places made with hands, which are the figures of the true; but into heaven itself, now to appear in the presence of God for us."

Jesus Christ is our intercessor. He is our great High Priest. He is also our standby by the help of the Holy Spirit. There is boldness in prayer. You are not thinking about "no" for an answer. You must know the will of God before you pray.

God planned your life. We came here when God finished on the sixth day. The only thing we met God doing was resting. Why? Because God did not want us to know how to struggle. Rest in the Bible means finished, or complete. The only way to enter into rest is through faith.

God determines us to be a success story before we were ever born. Ephesians 1:3: "Blessed be the God and Father of our Lord Jesus Christ, who hath blessed us with all spiritual blessings in heavenly places in Christ."

David discovered that you are fearfully and wonderfully made, so don't care what others feel about you.

Jesus said you are not just a living soul, but a living spirit.

You must have faith in your potential. If you keep the faith, you will truly become all God desired you to be. In Jesus Name. Shalom.

CHAPTER 4

Victory Over Death
(No Premature death)

The Lord's desire is to satisfy His Children with long life. However, we see many Christians not live long enough to fulfill their destiny. The Bible says in Hosea 4:6, "My people are destroyed for a lack of knowledge." It doesn't say that they are destroyed because they don't go to church or because they don't read the Bible or because the devil is wicked. God says in Hosea 4:6, "My people are destroyed for lack of knowledge."

God's people: born again, tongue-talking, holy ghost-filled Christians are destroyed by lack of knowledge because they have "rejected knowledge, [God] will also reject [them]." God is not saying that it is His plan to destroy His, nor is it His agenda. It is never His program. He loves His children with an everlasting love. But, because they have ignored His instructions, the enemy has caught up with them, hence, His people are destroyed for lack of knowledge. Every time you have an adequate knowledge about an issue of life from the Word of God, you can bring that issue to an end.

For example, tithing. By having an understanding from what God's Word says about tithing, you can stop poverty in your life. You can stop sickness and disease by knowing what God's word says about it. You defeat the fear of hell because you know that God's word says that if you confess with your mouth, and believe in your heart, you shall be saved. None of us saw an angel when we gave our life to Jesus. We believe it because God said it. Nothing physically changed in us as an indication that we were saved; regardless, you tell people you are born again and that you are a child of God. You know you are born again because God's Word said it.

God's word said something about longevity— if you don't know it, Satan will cheat you. The Bible says, "My people are destroyed because of lack of knowledge." Isaiah 5:13 says, "Therefore my people are gone into captivity because they have no knowledge, and their honorable men are famished and their multitude dried up with dust." This was not God's program. He didn't want His people to be in such bad condition—dried up and dusty, and famished. He didn't want them to be taken over by poverty, but they lacked knowledge of how to be free from such disasters.

Isaiah 5:14: (NASB) "Therefore Sheol has enlarged its throat and opened its mouth without measure; And Jerusalem's splendor, her multitude, her din of revelry and the jubilant within her, descend into it." Why was it that hell took over the destiny of God's precious people? Because they didn't have the knowledge of what it takes to be free of such calamity.

The problem is lack of knowledge. If you have the fear of untimely death, you are in bondage. If the fear of death rules your live, you will have no enjoyment of life. I have seen believers living as if they don't even know when death comes. God's word will show you that you don't have to be in bondage of the fear of death by knowing what it takes to live a life free of such fear.

The Bible says in Hebrews 2:14-15: "Forasmuch then as the children are partakers of flesh and blood, he also himself likewise took part of the same; that through death he might destroy him that had the power of death, that is, the devil; and deliver them who through fear of death were all their lifetime subject to bondage."

Death. Fear of pre-mature death is bondage and my people are destroyed because of lack of knowledge; therefore, they are in captivity. Fear of death is bondage if you don't know what it takes to be free from it. You will remain under that chain until you discover the secret of what it takes to be free, no matter how born again you are.

There is provision in God's word that terminates the power of pre-mature dead and untimely death. How so? Because from the beginning, death was not planned. In the agenda of the Almighty God, from Genesis chapter one, death can't be found on the list of all things God created. Death came as an interruption in the original plan of God. Man invited death. God did not invite death.

Genesis 2:15-17: And the Lord God took the man, and put him into the garden of Eden to dress it and to keep it. And the Lord God commanded the man, saying, of every tree of the garden thou mayest freely eat: but of the tree of the knowledge of good and evil, thou shalt not eat of it: for in the day that thou eatest thereof thou shalt surely die.

Here we see who brought death—Man. In fact, the birth of death is at the commission of man's disobedience. Death was not in the garden at all. Death needed man to create it because God didn't create death.

Henry Ford, by the wisdom God gave him, made a car. Henry Ford created and manufactured a car, but he did not create car accidents. But people die because of car accidents. Do we blame Henry Ford for their death because he made a car? Of course not. The driver is to be blamed.

God did not create death. Man brought death into the scene. When death came and poisoned man, the essence of Jesus' coming was to purge death out of man's system. Redemption is incomplete if you are not living free of the fear of death. Therefore, man is not permitted to die until he has accomplished his assignment on earth.

God's Word revealed to me that believers do not die because death does not have power over them. When you understand that you are not supposed to die young or prematurely based on what God's word says, you can begin to enjoy your redemption. Believers do not die. We don't.

I've told my church members that if their parents are attending this church, you better go to work, because if you are waiting for inheritance, by the time they are gone, it will be obsolete. If you are waiting to get their cars and houses, by the time they are gone, the house will be so old that you won't want it. I say you better go work right now because that man or woman is not dying, even if you pray.

1 Thessalonians 4:13-15: But I would not have you to be ignorant, brethren, concerning them which are asleep, that ye sorrow not, even as others which have no hope. For if we believe that Jesus died and rose again, even so them also which sleep in Jesus will God bring with him. For this we say unto you by the word of the Lord, that we which are alive and remain unto the coming of the Lord shall not prevent them which are asleep.

Ignorance is the problem. Would you cry if someone in your house was sleeping? The same mystery is made known to us in 1 Corinthians 15:51: "Behold, I shew you a mystery; We shall not all sleep, but we shall all be changed." The Bible also talks about David as asleep with his fathers. Also, Jesus, when He heard that Lazarus was dead exclaimed that Lazarus was sleeping. The reason the Bible talks about sleeping instead of death is because you don't sleep until you finished your assignment or are tired. The Bible says that people who sleep, sleep in the night. You sleep when you are finished; you sleep when you are tired.

CHAPTER 5

You Can Stay Healthy

You can have a sickness free life. You can stay healthy all the days of your life.

Psalms 105:36-37: "He smote also all the firstborn in their land, the chief of all their strength. He brought them forth with silver and gold, and there was not one feeble person among their tribes."

If it were possible for God to make sound health possible to over three million people for forty years, it is possible that, in your body, there won't be a trace of sickness. The way to stay healthy is made known to us in the word of God.

Sickness is spiritual. Therefore, sickness is healed spiritually. God never dealt with sickness in the physical. You have to remember that sickness and disease is spiritual, then you will have an idea of how to deal with it. Because if it is truly spiritual, then it must be healed by the word of God. He said, Psalm 107:20: "He sent His Word and healed them." When the Bible says, Isaiah 53:5: "He was wounded for our transgressions, and bruised for our iniquities," don't you see that this is also spiritual? "The chastisement of our peace was upon him; and with his stripes we are healed." I am repeating this over and over, because you must see that none of this is physical. It is all spiritual. If you read the rest of this chapter from that perspective, you will surely know that you never have to be sick. You can stay healthy.

Galatians 3:13-14, "Christ hath redeemed us from the curse of the law, being made a curse for us: for it is written, Cursed is everyone that hangeth on a tree: That the blessing of Abraham might come on the Gentiles through Jesus Christ; that we might receive the promise of the Spirit through faith."

When the curse came upon the earth, it put everyone in bondage. You need to understand what the curse is, how it comes, and how to get out of it. Ignorance on these three points will make it impossible for you to know how to escape.

The curse of the law is poverty, sickness and disease, and spiritual death, all of which came upon humanity through the disobedience of Adam. Deuteronomy 28:15, 59-60: "(15) But it shall come to pass, if thou wilt not hearken unto the voice of the Lord thy God, to observe to do all his commandments and his statutes which I command thee this day; that all these curses shall come upon thee, and overtake thee." (This is where it all started) "(59-60) Then the Lord will make thy plagues wonderful, and the plagues of thy seed, even great plagues, and of long continuance, and sore sicknesses, and of long continuance. Moreover He will bring upon thee all the diseases of Egypt, which thou wast afraid of; and they shall cleave unto thee."

Sickness is one of the major curses of the law. Scriptures will help you better understand the effect of the curse are found in Deuteronomy 28:21-27: "The Lord shall make the pestilence cleave unto thee, until He have consumed thee from off the land, whither thou goest to possess it. The Lord shall smite thee with a consumption [tuberculosis], and with a fever, and with an inflammation, and with an extreme burning, and with the sword, and with blasting, and with mildew; and they shall pursue thee until thou perish. And thy heaven that is over thy head shall be brass, and the earth that is under thee shall be iron. The Lord shall make the rain of thy land powder and dust: from heaven shall it come down upon thee, until thou be destroyed. The Lord shall cause thee to be smitten before thine enemies: thou shalt go out one way against them, and flee seven ways before them: and shalt be removed into all the kingdoms of the earth. And thy carcase shall be meat unto all fowls of the air, and unto the beasts of the earth, and no man shall fray them away.[27] The Lord will smite thee with the botch of Egypt, and with the emerods, and with the scab, and with the itch, whereof thou canst not be healed. The Lord shall smite thee with madness, and blindness, and astonishment of heart: And thou shalt grope at noonday, as the blind gropeth in darkness, and thou shalt not prosper in thy ways: and thou shalt be only oppressed and spoiled evermore, and no man shall save thee. Thou shalt betroth a wife, and another man shall lie with her: thou shalt build an house, and thou shalt not dwell therein: thou shalt plant a vineyard, and shalt not gather the grapes thereof."

These ailments came because of the curse. It is true that sickness and disease can come through sin; however, a person can live a holy life and still get sick. Why? It is not because of the sins the person committed which caused the sickness; it is because of the original sin that we inherited from Adam and Eve.

The escape from sickness and diseases is in the provision that God made in Christ Jesus. If you don't appropriate the provisions, despite living a holy life, the enemy, the devil, will afflict you with sickness. It is the devil who makes sure that when the curse is released, it is affected.

God does not put curses on people. However, when we walk in disobedience, or when we walk against the law of God, the devil goes into action to make sure those curses stay upon our lives. The devil uses the curse to bring sickness and disease, affliction, premature death, in the lives of people.

Luke 13:10-16: And He was teaching in one of the synagogues on the sabbath. And, behold, there was a woman which had a spirit of infirmity eighteen years, and was bowed together, and could in no wise lift up herself. And when Jesus saw her, He called her to him, and said unto her, Woman, thou art loosed from thine infirmity. And He laid his hands on her: and immediately she was made straight, and glorified God. And the ruler of the synagogue answered with indignation, because that Jesus had healed on the sabbath day, and said unto the people, There are six days in which men ought to work: in them therefore come and be healed, and not on the sabbath day. The Lord then answered him, and said, Thou hypocrite, doth not each one of you on the sabbath loose his ox or his ass from the stall, and lead him away to watering? And ought not this woman, being a daughter of Abraham, whom Satan hath bound, lo, these eighteen years, be loosed from this bond on the sabbath day?

Satan was the force behind that woman sickness.

Isaiah 14:12-17: How art thou fallen from heaven, O Lucifer, son of the morning! how art thou cut down to the ground, which didst weaken the nations! For thou hast said in thine heart, I will ascend into heaven, I will exalt my throne above the stars of God: I will sit also upon the mount of the congregation, in the sides of the north: I will ascend above the heights of the clouds; I will be like the most High. Yet thou shalt be brought down to hell, to the sides of the pit. They that see thee shall narrowly look upon thee, and consider thee, saying, Is this the man that made the earth to tremble, that did shake kingdoms; That made the world as a wilderness, and destroyed the cities thereof; that opened not the house of his prisoners?

The devil wants to steal, kill, and destroy. Sickness and disease is a type of prison which limits people from doing what they want to do. It scatters their dreams.

Jesus Christ came and redeemed us from the curse. To be redeemed means to be bought over. Jesus Christ bought you over from Satan. As a believer, you are exempted from sickness for Christ has redeemed you, In other words, you are paid for.

1 John 3:8: He that committeth sin is of the devil; for the devil sinneth from the beginning. For this purpose the Son of God was manifested, that He might destroy the works of the devil.

The works of the devil that make people sick have been destroyed. The work that is putting people in prison have been destroyed also. To live in the victory of Jesus Christ, you must know: 1) that God has delivered you from the works of Satan, and 2) how to appropriate the provision of your deliverance.

Unfortunately, many believers accept sickness and disease as a form of God's training weapon. They refuse to fight sickness so as not to tamper with the will of God. If fighting sickness is tampering with the will of God, then why are you taking medicine? Why are you sinning against God by taking medicine? Sickness is from the devil. Jesus Christ came to destroy that work. If you know and agree that Jesus Christ died and rose from the dead for you, then sickness is already destroyed as far as you are concern.

Colossians 2:14-15: Blotting out the handwriting of ordinances that was against us, which was contrary to us, and took it out of the way, nailing it to his cross; And having spoiled principalities and powers, He made a shew of them openly, triumphing over them in it.

To stay healthy all the days of your life, you must understand God's position on the matter. Being born again will not preclude you from the attack of Satan. It is your responsibility to know what to tell the devil when he brings sickness. When you hear that someone is sick, know that the devil is sending a message to you too. The devil is like a sale person in the market. If he comes to you and you reject his product, he packs up and goes to someone else. If you keep your mouth shut, he sets up the display table and begins to show you his products. The devil doesn't have access to your body until you let your guard down. Your body is important to God to the extent that there is a department, set in the kingdom of God, called the department of healing. If anything is wrong with your body, Jesus Christ takes it upon Himself to come and heal you. As powerful as God is, He can't come to you to do anything without a license from you.

Many times, I have faced challenges with my health. I disallowed sickness in my body by making use of the provisions for my health which God made available to me in His Son Jesus Christ. If you say one thing and do something else, you are deceiving yourself, not God, and you are opening the door for the enemy.

Here are cardinal principles to apply to your live to stay in perfect health:

1) Apply the blood. One of the weapons for destroying curses is the blood of Jesus Christ. The plague of sickness released by the devil cannot cross the blood line. Even if the plague is all around you, when it comes to where the blood is, it must cease.

   God told Moses He couldn't guarantee every life in the city unless He saw the blood. If any Israelite refused to put the blood on the doorpost they would die. Every Israelite escaped death because they applied the blood.

The cause of every curse is sin. The foundation for every curse is sin. The medication for every sin is the blood. Hebrews 9:22, "And almost all things are by the law purged with blood; and without shedding of blood is no remission." God couldn't forgive anyone until the blood was applied. Sin is more powerful than sickness. Sickness get its strength from sin. If Adam and Eve hadn't fallen, we wouldn't be talking about sickness.

Sin is eliminated when the blood of Jesus is applied. Anytime sickness appears on your body, take hold of the blood. The enemy put people in the prison of sickness to kill them. Zechariah 9:11, "As for thee also, by the blood of thy covenant I have sent forth thy prisoners out of the pit wherein is no water." If the devil puts you in the pit, there is a way out, through the blood of Jesus Christ. The devil puts his victims in the pit to keep them completely out of God's program for their lives.

If your health is in the pit, apply the blood by testifying to yourself what God says the blood of Jesus has done for you. Leviticus 17:11, "For the life of the flesh is in the blood: and I have given it to you upon the altar to make an atonement for your souls: for it is the blood that maketh an atonement for the soul." And John 1:4-5, "In him was life; and the life was the light of men. And the light shineth in darkness; and the darkness comprehended it not."

In the blood of Jesus is the life of God, and that life is the light which, wherever it shines, sickness and disease being the work of darkness, disappears. Anytime you, by faith, apply the blood of Jesus with your mouth, the light of God shines in the midst of darkness and destroys sickness.

There is no such thing as hereditary diseases or sickness in the body of a born-again child of God. Acts 17:28, "For in him we live, and move, and have our being; as certain also of your own poets have said, For we are also his offspring." In natural birth, you are related to your parents; however, you are God's offspring. If you belong to God, then you don't carry the gene of men.

2 Corinthians 5:17, "Therefore if any man be in Christ, He is a new creature: old things are passed away; behold, all things are become new." Anyone in Christ Jesus is a new being. A new being! Your family gene is now God's. The spiritual birth makes conception the natural birth but the fatherhood changes. The day Jesus Christ died and rose from the dead, the pregnancy started. The day you receive Him, you are born. When you accepted Jesus Christ into your life, that was the day of delivery. Therefore, in Him you live and move and have your being. For it to take effect in your life, you must believe it, and act it. Take the blood by faith.

The meaning of communion is you eat the flesh of Jesus Christ and drink His blood, His physical blood, by faith. That's the blood of God you are drinking. It only works by faith. Sadly, many believers do not know this truth. That's why they take communion ritually as a church rite. Revelation 12:11, "And they overcame him by the blood of the Lamb, and by the word of their testimony; and they loved not their lives unto the death." The instrument of their victory was the blood and confession. Confession means saying the same thing God said. Or repeating after God. For everything the devil has done, God has given us the blood of His Son to undo it.

2) Curse the curse. The language that a curse understand is the curse. Curse it. If you are too lenient and polite with the devil, he will make you his best friend. In Genesis

12:3, God said to Abraham, "…I will bless them that bless thee, and curse him that curseth thee; and in thee shall all families of the earth be blessed." So, one of the medications for curses is a curse.

You must understand that you are not an ordinary person. There is fire in your tongue. God said, "I have given you a mouth and a wisdom which none of your adversary will be able to resist or gainsay nor resist." What you say, by the authority of God, becomes a law.

Luke 9:1: "Then He called his twelve disciples together, and gave them power and authority over all devils, and to cure diseases." There are two very important points in this passage. The Lord said, "…what I say unto [one] I say unto all…" (Mark 13:37).

Power is an ability to get work done. Authority is an institution. You can only be empowered with authority. When you are in authority, you are not speaking by your influence alone—you are speaking with the influence of a higher power. God said, "I gave unto you power, and I give you authority, so when you speak forget about you, for it's not your power, but your authority, that will get the job done. "It has nothing to do with you. It has everything to do with God. Anything that wants to resist your words will have to ultimately resist the person who empowered you. Therefore, in speaking to sickness and disease, such as cancer, say, "Die, in the name of Jesus Christ," and leave it between Jesus and the cancer.

The Greek word for authority is exousia. The prefix "ex" means "out." Exousia, something that comes out, e.g., exodus. Jesus Christ, in giving power and authority to His disciples, expected them to see it by faith, as it was not something tangible. You can't see authority. You can't see power. But you have it.

Once, as a young believer in the faith, I attended a powerful, impactful meeting where I encountered teachings I didn't know were in the Bible. We were taught that we can cast out demons. I was shocked. I asked, "How could that be possible?" In my original doctrinal background of Baptist, such believes were considered unbiblical. I was amazed by the speaker. He sat in a corner of the room and commanded demons to come out of people. Even the person who took me to the meeting, a pastor, and his wife, got delivered from demoniacal influence.

When I got home that day, I decided to act on what I had learned. When I hear a truth, I will practice it to know if it is true or not. My sister was sick with an ulcer. When I got home, I began to pray for her. I laid my hand on her, and said, "In the name of Jesus, come out!"

My sister had the same reaction I witnessed in the people to whom the man at the meeting ministered. I wasn't expecting it. My sister began to manifest the presence of something. I didn't know much then. I was just trying to practice what I had seen. I didn't know what to do. I stopped praying and sat my sister on a chair, panicked, but she continued to manifest. There was no one in the house to help me.

I began to apologize. I said, "I'm sorry, I won't do it again." But it was too late. She continued to manifest the same way as had happened in the meeting. I ran outside to get help, but there was no one anywhere near. I started to blame myself for being prideful, afraid that my pride would kill my sister. If I were not prideful, I wouldn't have been so bold. I was scared. I didn't know what to do at all. I said, "Lord, if you deliver me from this, I will never try this again."

I came back inside and my sister was still manifesting. With the last strength I had (I believe it was the Holy Spirit helping me even though I didn't know Him then as I do now), I said, "In the name of Jesus, you demon, come out!"

My sister vomited, and then immediately stood up and cleaned herself. In amazement, I asked her how she felt. She said, "The thing just came."

In a moment of bravado, I said, "I told you! I told you before, I know Jesus Christ can do anything. If you have any friend who may need similar help…" But, inside, I was saying please don't bring anyone else.

After this experience, courage came over me. I began to look for anyone who needed deliverance. I didn't know the power was there all along. This happened to me when I was a few weeks old in the faith. I don't know your age in the faith, but the power is there for you, too. Curse the curse.

In Mark 11:12-14, Jesus Christ cursed the fig tree by saying "no one will eat out of you anymore forever." His disciples heard it. The following day, His disciples saw the tree dried up from the root. Jesus Christ admonished them that they could do the same thing if they exercise the same kind of faith.

Curse the root of sickness and disease. To whatever that is not working well in your body, say, "I curse you, get out, in the name of Jesus!" That is the language it understands. God says He has anointed you with power and authority. You can curse whatever is not producing in your life, for God is not the author of it.

3) Stay in the covenant. As long as you stay in the covenant, you are covered and secured.

Numbers 23:7-8: And He took up his parable, and said, Balak the king of Moab hath brought me from Aram, out of the mountains of the east, saying, Come, curse me Jacob, and come, defy Israel. How shall I curse, whom God hath not cursed? or how shall I defy, whom the Lord hath not defied?

You are not cursed by God. I repeat, you are not cursed by God. Satan is too small to place a curse on you. Sickness is a curse. However, you must remain in the covenant of God to be exempted from the curse of the original sin. Do not step out of the covenant. If you step out of the covenant, your life is exposed to anything the enemy wants to do. God will always respect His covenant over the life of His people to make sure no evil happens to them, because if it does, it becomes a slap to His integrity.

Psalms 74:20: "Have respect unto the covenant: for the dark places of the earth are full of the habitations of cruelty." God will always have respect for the covenant. Only the covenant of God will single you out of the many wickedness on the earth. You stay in the covenant by doing the bidding of the covenant. The bidding of the covenant is this: Matthew 22:37-40: "Jesus said unto him, Thou shalt love the Lord thy God with all thy heart, and with all thy soul, and with all thy mind. This is the first and great commandment. And the second is like unto it, Thou shalt love thy neighbour as thyself. On these two commandments hang all the law and the prophets."

4) Make a choice to be healthy. Make a choice to stay in health.

Deuteronomy 30:19: I call heaven and earth to record this day against you, that I have set before you life and death, blessing and cursing: therefore choose life, that both thou and thy seed may live.

Sound health is a choice. If you don't decide unequivocally to be healthy, it's proof you are not ready to be in health. You must keep on telling yourself, "I make a choice to be blessed."

It is impossible to choose health without knowing the provision for health in the word. One of the provisions for your health is Isaiah 33:24: "And the inhabitant shall not say, I am sick: the people that dwell therein shall be forgiven their iniquity."

God of heaven and the earth says we should not say we are sick. That's a choice. If you say something contrary, then you are speaking against your health. Say what God said you should say—this is what is meant by confession. He said I shall not say I am sick, so I'm not sick, according to the word of God in Isaiah 33:24.

He said, "By His stripes, I am healed." Isaiah 53:5. So, according to the word of God, by the stripes of Jesus Christ, I am healed. I am well. I am not sick. Knowing the provision in the word of God for your health, emboldens you and gives you a fighting spirit to attack the devil.

James 4:7: "Submit yourselves therefore to God. Resist the devil, and he will flee from you." One of the tricks of the enemy is to make the sickness seem more powerful and bigger than you.

1 John 4:4, "Ye are of gods, little children, and have overcome them: because greater is He that is in you, than he that is in the world." No matter the degree of sickness that comes against you, you are still bigger and stronger than that sickness. The enemy is going to try to demoralize you to get you to submit to him in the sickness. Don't yield for a second. There is no sickness or name, here on earth, that is not under you. Greater is He that is in you than any

sickness or disease in the world. This ought to always be your thinking and speaking.

The only medication without side effects is the word of God. You can't overdose on God's word. The Bible says the word of God is medicine to your flesh (Proverb 4:22). Knowing what the word of God says about you will destroy and keep the devil out of your life permanently.

CHAPTER 6

Sound Health

"God's Will For You"

Sickness, disease, affliction and oppression of any kind is an affront against the finished work of Jesus Christ. It is against God's covenant with His Son, Jesus Christ, of whom you are a direct benefactor, if you have given your life to Jesus Christ. God does not use ailments of any kind to train His children.

If affliction does not come from God, from whom do they come? The enemy, satan. It is your responsibility to reject anything which God did not send. The kingdom of God has enough provision for the earth and all the citizens to make sure that none are sick. The stripes on the body of our Lord Jesus is that provision; it is the medication for your health.

The death of our Lord Jesus was both spiritual and physical. The reason the Lord Jesus was given thirty-nine lashes was that, by the plan of the Almighty, those stripes were to be for your healing, for your peace to be established.

We see this truth in Isaiah 53: 1-6: Who hath believed our report? and to whom is the arm of the Lord revealed? For He shall grow up before him as a tender plant, and as a root out of a dry ground: He hath no form nor comeliness; and when we shall see him, there is no beauty that we should desire him. He is despised and rejected of men; a man of sorrows, and acquainted with grief:

and we hid as it were our faces from him; He was despised, and we esteemed him not. Surely He hath borne our griefs, and carried our sorrows: yet we did esteem him stricken, smitten of God, and afflicted. But He was wounded for our transgressions, He was bruised for our iniquities: the chastisement of our peace was upon him; and with his stripes we are healed. All we like sheep have gone astray; we have turned everyone to his own way; and the Lord hath laid on him the iniquity of us all."

The reason many people remain afflicted, diseased, and sick, is due to their unwillingness to believe the report of heaven. People choose to believe the hospital report and the feeling of their body rather than the heavenly message that by the stripes of Jesus Christ they were healed. The price to obtain peace from diabetes, leukemia, cancer, or whatever ailment, was paid by the stripes of Jesus Christ. If any sickness, by whatever name it may be called, is happening in your life, it is incumbent upon you to make demand of the stripes, for by the stripes, you are healed.

Just as there are laws which govern natural affairs and processes of man, there are spiritual laws which govern spiritual realities. There is a law in the Kingdom of God which forbids sickness and diseases, made known in Exodus 23:25-26: "And ye shall serve the Lord your God, and He shall bless thy bread, and thy water; and I will take sickness away from the midst of thee. There shall nothing cast their young, nor be barren, in thy land: the number of thy days I will fulfil." The Lord said, most emphatically, "I will take sickness away from the midst of thee." He took sickness from the midst of His children on the cross. If you hear rumors of sicknesses and diseases spreading where you are, only believe on the cross. He took those things from you.

Salvation without sound health is an incomplete salvation. Jesus Christ is the savior of our soul as much as He is the savior of our body. Your soul being saved and your body being sick is unacceptable to God. So, don't accept it.

Ephesians 5:23: "For the husband is the head of the wife, even as Christ is the head of the church: and He is the savior of the body."

The moment you gave your life to Jesus Christ, your soul was saved. At the coming of the Lord Jesus Christ, you shall reign with Him, as long as you meet the condition stated in the word of God—by faith you are saved. The Savior of your soul is also the Savior of your body. As you are confident that your soul is saved, by the word of God, express the same confidence that your body is saved too, for Jesus Christ paid the price both for your soul and your body. Do not take the salvation of your soul and leave the salvation of your body behind.

Often, physical ailments originate in the mind. The enemy paints a picture of what could be wrong. The enemy makes you receive it by thinking about it. The moment it has a root in your thinking pattern, you may not get deliverance using fasting and praying. The enemy will wire the thought of what you are feeling in your body and to establish the symptoms firmly in your mind. This is how the spirit of infirmity takes over a person, exemplifying Proverb 23:7: "As a man thinketh in his heart so is He."

If your thinking pattern conforms to the suggestions of the enemy, it becomes difficult for God to intervene. He can only intervene with His word. A believer needs to renew his or her mind according to the word of God by saying and thinking the same things that God says concerning sickness and disease so that sickness and disease will not have a grip over their life. Many born-again believers are sickly because they don't have redemptive thinking, patterned after God's word. The thinking pattern of a believer should be according to Philippians 4:8: "Finally, brethren, whatsoever things are true, whatsoever things are honest, whatsoever things are just, whatsoever things are pure, whatsoever things are lovely, whatsoever things are of good report; if there be any virtue, and if there be any praise, think on these things." So, if what's going on in your life does not fall into any of these categories, discard it. Don't sit on it in thought.

Understand this: fact and truth are not the same thing. Medical reports give facts about what is happening, has happened, or will happen in the body; the truth is what God says. The truth does not originate from the laboratory but from the Word of God. The facts can be changed. God's Word cannot change. The application of the truth to the fact changes the fact to the truth. How do we apply truth to facts? By saying with our mouth and believing with our heart what God has said concerning the problem, situation, or circumstances.

Philippians 4:8 gives us a thinking pattern on which to structure our thought-life. For example, a medical report is given to you. According to Philippians 4:8, how should you think about the report? 1) "Whatsoever things are true." The medical report is factual truth validated by medical experts. However, your thinking should be, "What does God say concerning this?" Is it true, according to the word of God, that this medical report is indeed God's original design and function of your body? If not, then reject it, in the name of Jesus Christ. 2) "Whatsoever things are honest." If the report is an accurate portrayal of your body, as created by God, and redeemed by the blood of Jesus Christ, then it is honest. 3) "Whatsoever things are just." Another word for "just" is "righteous." Is the statement of report you had from the hospital righteous? 4) "Whatsoever things are pure." There is no sickness or disease that is pure, as the Bible calls disease fowl spirits. 5) "Whatsoever things are lovely." I have never seen anybody who enjoys sickness. There is nothing amiable about sickness. 6) "Whatsoever things are of good report." Bad medical diagnosis does not provoke praise or thanksgiving. 7) "If there be any virtue. If there be any praise, think on these things." Virtue and Praise is found only in the word of God.

The admonition of God is that you ought to think only His word in every situation. Think God's word, always. Refuse to think the prevailing opinions. God says, whatsoever is true, honest, pure, lovely—think on those things. Many believers are trying to figure it out on their own, and they end up failing miserably. They need to receive strength on the inside from the Lord Jesus. And then, by the help of the Holy Spirit in the inner man, their thought patterns will begin to conform to the word of God. The key is to keep on saying the same thing God says.

Sound health is your inheritance in Christ Jesus, however, you will only experience sound health through the understanding of the kingdom provisions and the steps that are expected of you.

What you need to know to receive sound health from God are:

1. You need to know God loves you. If you don't fully understand God's love, receiving from Him may prove difficult. Unfortunately, religion has given believers a negative image of God. God has been portrayed as vengeful, angry, ready-to-punish father who is just waiting for His children to messed up so He can give them sickness and disease.

That. Is. Not. God. God is your father. He hates sickness, disease, or pain of any kind. He poured His love on you at Calvary. Think of it this way: the prize of a thing determines its worth. If you want something of lasting value, you must be prepared to pay the price.

1 Peter 1:18-19: Forasmuch as ye know that ye were not redeemed with corruptible things, as silver and gold, from your vain conversation received by tradition from your fathers; But with the precious blood of Christ, as of a lamb without blemish and without spot.

The price determines the worth. We were all in the slave market, sold out to sin, and were subject in the camp of the government of Satan to do whatever he wanted with us. For a slave to be free, he or she must pay for that freedom, or someone must buy the slave's freedom. God says the price for our freedom from slavery was not silver and gold. God looked at us and considered us worth more than silver and gold, so He sent His Son as the worth of your life. Your life is priced by the life of God.

If you have a million dollars and want to purchase a product worth a million dollars, that money ceased to be of value to you because the product which you want to buy is worth more to you than the money. The moment God released Jesus to the cross, He stopped thinking about Him; the next thing Jesus said was, "My God, my God, why has thou forsaken me!"

You cost God everything. So, don't ever doubt His love. If you cost God everything, why would God be delighted to see you sick, depressed, cast down, downtrodden? Whatever maybe happening in your body, in your life, know that love covered all of it. God giving His Son is proof of His commitment to your health.

2. Put your faith to work. Faith is not based on feeling nor sensory perception. Kingdom faith is based on the Word.

2 Corinthians 5:7: "For we walk by faith, not by sight."

If you depend on your feelings, you won't obtain sound health. The same thing is shown in Mark 11:23-24: "For verily I say unto you, That whosoever shall say unto this mountain, Be thou removed, and be thou cast into the sea; and shall not doubt in his heart, but shall believe that those things which He saith shall come to pass; He shall have whatsoever He saith. Therefore I say unto you, What things soever ye desire, when ye pray, believe that ye receive them, and ye shall have them." Many believers do not receive what they pray for because they want to feel it first, and then believe they have received. God says you must believe first, then you will receive.

A case in point is when the Lord Jesus cursed the fig tree and walked away. As far as He was concerned, the fig tree was dead, even though when He walked away, it still had green leaves. The Lord Jesus Christ did not go back to inspect the fig tree. His disciples called His attention to it.

The Lord walked by faith. He didn't have to go back to check to see if it had come to pass. You need to learn this valuable lesson: The fact that you are still feeling the pain does not mean you are not healed. God's word is the determinant of your health.

Many want to see their healing first, then they believe. They will never be healed. It doesn't work that way. Believe. Receive. In that order. Think and speak this way, "Jesus Christ has already healed me. I know it, for He said so in His word. Even though I'm still experiencing symptoms, I will not think on the feelings. I believe I am healed. I receive it, in Jesus name!" If you receive the word of God, then you receive the one who spoke it, then every sickness will follow your faith and leave your body. This kind of faith does not come simply by hearing the Word, but by meditating on the Word, and letting it sink into your spirit. This kind of faith is not only for sound health, but for every area of your life. Learning to generate this kind of faith will reveal to you who God is, and from that revelation comes an intimidate understanding of the Word of God.

3. Understand your healing. Your health was perfected when Jesus fulfilled His assignment on earth. Jesus Christ came to earth to restore God's family to its original form. Redemption, the finished work of Jesus Christ, is all about going back to the Garden of Eden. Jesus Christ said in John 6:38, "For I came down from heaven, not to do mine own will, but the will of him that sent me." In Luke 4:18, He also said, "The Spirit of the Lord is upon me, because He hath anointed me to preach the gospel to the poor; He hath sent me to heal the brokenhearted, to preach deliverance to the captives, and recovering of sight to the blind, to set at liberty them that are bruised."

What do you think would be good news to a poor person? Money, wealth? A poor person does not need any other news. Within the prophecy of Isaiah, God said to the poor, you are going to be rich. Jesus Christ became poor that you may become rich through His poverty.

The prophet also said, "He hath sent me to heal the brokenhearted." When people are broken on the inside, everything is broken down because "as a man thinketh in his heart, so is he."

The prophet also said, "...to preach deliverance to the captives..." This is sickness and disease. Sickness and disease are in the category of bondage. In Job 42:10, the Bible says, "...and God turned the captivity of Job when he prayed for his friend." The sickness and disease that came upon Job is recognized here as "captivity."

Acts 10:38 says, "How God anointed Jesus of Nazareth with the Holy Ghost and power, who went about doing good and healing all that were oppressed of the devil; for God was with him." Jesus Christ came to destroy sickness and disease from holding men and women captive. When you call upon Jesus to touch your body, you are giving heaven an opportunity to fulfill the ministry of Jesus. Knowing your right, as a child of God in Christ Jesus, not only exempts you from wickedness, it also equips you with a ready answer for when the enemy comes.

I heard a story of a man, who is now in glory, who pastored for twenty years and never buried a single member; not because people did not get sick, but because he had taught them how to live in health.

Matthew 8:16-17: When the even was come, they brought unto him many that were possessed with devils: and He cast out the spirits with his word, and healed all that were sick: That it might be fulfilled which was spoken by Esaias the prophet, saying, Himself took our infirmities, and bare our sicknesses.

The difference between take and took is that one is present tense, the other is past tense. Jesus Christ took (past tense) your sickness so, right now, you don't have any sickness whatsoever. He took it.

If I feel any form of symptom in my body, the first thing I do is repent. I apologize to God for stealing back from Him what He had taken from me. Perhaps I went somewhere, and unbeknownst to me, picked something up God didn't give me. I repent, immediately. Now that I know that God has forgiven me, I speak to the sickness, in the name of Jesus. I command it to leave me immediately. Even if the symptom is still there, I know God has heard me. I don't mind the symptom. I mind the word.

Do not let religion deceive you into thinking or believing that God is using sickness to train you into obedience or righteousness. Sickness does not come from God. Can God use sickness to bring about an outcome to the glory of His name? Yes. But He is not the one who originated the sickness. God does not delight in the suffering of His children. You will not see that anywhere in His word. Do not let anyone teach you otherwise.

4. Recognize the healing engine in you. The blessed Holy Spirit is in residence in every believer. There is a measure of the Holy Spirit inside every born-again child of God.

Romans 8:11: But if the Spirit of him that raised up Jesus from the dead dwell in you, He that raised up Christ from the dead shall also quicken your mortal bodies by his Spirit that dwelleth in you.

This passage does not refer to the resurrection of the body. It is talking about the body you now occupy being made whole by the spirit of God who lives in you. The word "quicken" means to make alive. The Spirit of God inside of you wants to bring life back to dead tissues and organs in your body. The Spirit brings life back to your system even when it has gone down. The Spirit which raised the Lord Jesus from the dead is in you right now to bring life back into your system. Just like The Spirit raised Jesus from the dead, He is ready to raise you from the bed of sickness.

Matthew 12:28: But if I cast out devils by the Spirit of God, then the kingdom of God is come unto you.

The Spirit of the living God, who worked in Jesus Christ to expel demons from people, is the same Spirit that is now in you. By faith, you can ask, "Holy Spirit, thank you for dwelling in me. I appreciate your presence. Precious Holy Spirit flow to (any area of your body experiencing any symptom), in the name of Jesus, quicken my hand, quicken my liver." Then thank Him for healing you, for quickening your mortal body.

Out of your belly shall flow rivers of living water. Direct the water to where you need it. Not just in your body but in every aspect of life. You must declare war on sickness, to live in health. Declare the war of faith. Faith comes by hearing, and by hearing the word of Christ. You must renew your mind daily with the word of Christ to maintain the stamina of your faith. Even while being sick, challenges even more struggling will arise to challenge your faith. Constantly build up your faith. Stay in God's presence to receive a fresh fire daily.

CHAPTER 7

Why God Heals

The most exciting time for our members at Christ Resurrection Power Assembly is our anniversary. But the anniversary is not our celebration. It's not a celebration of "let's come together." No. An anniversary is a yearly event when we go to Shilo to meet with God.

For the next three-hundred sixty-five days, God will instruct each of us about the steps to take. That's why we come together. If it was only for food or a funfair, then we've failed. If it was only for dressing up, putting on our Sunday best, and greeting people, then we've failed. We can dress up any day of the week. We can go to the mall to greet people. This coming together is a time for an encounter.

"God, I am here this year. This is what needs to happen before next year." That's what we come for.

Israel never joked with their yearly appearance before God in Shilo. In fact, all of the families prepared for their appearance way in advance. If other things were planned for that time, they readily suspended them. They didn't joke with this, because they knew they were struggling and they wanted new strength.

When you go to Shilo, you never return the same. Rachel said to Jacob, "Give me a child lest I die." Jacob said, "There is nothing I can do, let's go to Shilo." If you go and appear before God at Shilo, He will do it.

God set it aside to meet with His people, and those days are wired from heaven. The problem is that we brought democracy to the Kingdom of God and it doesn't work here. It is only what the King says that holds.

Please don't waste the anointing that is coming from the eighteenth to the twenty-first century. Be desperate with all your heart. Don't leave your heart at home and carry your body here. Don't come because you want to attend; come because there must be a change. If you ask our members, they will confirm that each year there is a change in the ministry. That change has nothing to do with what we do. It is because our hearts are fixed with faith, expectation, and trust in God.

We belong in a Kingdom, and Jesus Christ said, "Thy will be done on earth as it is in heaven." The Kingdom of God on the earth must reflect what is in heaven.

Revelation 22:1-2: And He shewed me a pure river of water of life, clear as crystal, proceeding out of the throne of God and of the lamb. In the midst of the street of it, and on either side of the river, there was the tree of life, which bare twelve manners of fruits, and yielded her fruit every month; and the leaves of the tree were for the healing of the nations.

There are enough provisions in heaven for every month for every individual in heaven never to be sick. If that tree was to be removed from heaven, heaven would also be sick. Jesus said, "Thy will be done on earth as it is in heaven," and in heaven there is a tree that supplies health for every inhabitant of heaven. Every month, it has enough fruit to take care of the inhabitants. The Kingdom of God has a department responsible for health.

In Isaiah 33:24, God said, "And the inhabitant shall not say, I am sick; the people that dwell therein shall be forgiven their iniquity." I love the way the Good News translation puts it: "No one who lives in our land will ever again complain of being sick, and all sins will be forgiven."

Sickness was never part of God's program for us in Christ Jesus. A lot of people have been taught that God uses sickness to train people, but that is not true. Jeremiah 8:22 says, "Is there no balm in Gilead? Is there no physician there? Whey then is not the health of the daughter of my people recovered."

If God made provisions for their health, why are they still sick? Sickness is a poison. It's a poison to your health. There are enough provisions in the kingdom of God to destroy the poison that the enemy has injected into your system. The moment you understand this, you will be smiling when others talk about their illnesses because you know it has nothing to do with you.

In Numbers 21, after the Israelites sinned against God, a fiery serpent came into their camp and was biting them. It was biting them to the degree that they begin to die in thousands. In verse eight, God saw so many people were dying of all kinds of complications that came thru the poison of the serpent bite that He told Moses to make a serpent of brass and hang it on a pole, and whoever looked upon that serpent made of brass would be healed.

God can be humorous. That is why smart people die quick. God gives you every opportunity to argue with the Bible. You don't learn these things in the university. You learn it in the Word by the Spirit of God. What if someone told you that if you have a snake bite you should look up at a brass snake and you will be healed? The first thing you would say is "Oh, no. I am going to the emergency room." You would call an ambulance to make sure you got there before the poison spread. You wouldn't argue about going to the emergency room, but you would certainly argue about looking at the brass serpent for healing.

God gives you room to argue because He wants you to know that He is God. Anytime faith is released to God's Word, God performs wonders and miracles in the life of His people. Stop arguing with His Word.

Why does God Heals? Because of His Love.

God's love is unconditional. In my years of ministry, I have seen God heal people and I began to ask questions, but why because some people are more serious than others? If it was left up to me, I would ask God to allow me to line the sick people up and heal this person first, and maybe skip over that person because he or she is not serious about being healed.

But because God's love is unconditional, He responds to your faith. He heals you because He loves you and He can't stand for anything to touch you or mess up your life. Zechariah 2:8 says "he that touches you touches the apple of God's eyes." That is the same God that said "let there be light," and there was light.

God's love is overwhelming. He said in John 3:16, "For God so loved the world, that he gave his only begotten Son, that whosoever believeth in him should not perish, but have everlasting life". God didn't just love the church. He loved the world. But if you stop reading there, you won't be able to see the beauty of John 3:17: "For God sent not His Son into the world to condemn it, [the word condemn means to judge. When the word judge is used in the Bible, it means to kill. Remember the two thieves that were condemned? That is condemnation. It's crucifixion]. so that the world thru Him might be saved," as well as healed and justified.

I went to the hospital some years ago to visit a pastor. The pastor was sick and the medical personnel had already started an IV on him before I arrived. I asked the pastor, "What are you doing here?" He said, "Oh, I am sick." I said, "Come on now, let's get out of here. After all, the way this IV thing is just drip, drip, drip, it will take forever for it to get inside your body. Why don't they just give it to you in a cup to drink? Then we can go home." I said, "This is not the place where you are supposed to be." The minute I said it, that thing rushed into his spirit like a light from heaven. He said, "You are right. I'm out of here!" And He was instantly healed.

Why does God heal?.Because Your Body is His Temple

Don't let the Devil put fear into your heart. Stand your ground. God is with you. Your body is the temple of God. God said, "I will dwell in them and walk in them, and I will be their God, and they shall be My people." The Bible says we are the habitation of God through the spirit. If that is true, then it is impossible for God to be living in the same apartment with sickness. Light and darkness cannot stay together. There is enough anointing inside of you that can bring healing to your body if you will release that anointing.

Romans 8:11: But if the Spirit of Him that raised up Jesus from the dead dwell in you, He that raised up Christ from the dead shall also quicken your mortal bodies by His Spirit that dwelleth in you.

You are not living the life of the flesh, you are living the life of the spirit; If the Holy Spirit of God dwells within you, directs and controls you. But anyone that does not possess the Spirit of Christ is non of His. That person does not belong to Christ. He's not truly a child of God.

The Spirit of God quickens. The word "quickens" means bring to life. Some people mistakenly believe that scripture means that the Spirit of the Lord is going to quicken us when we get to heaven. No. Mortal means dead. The Holy Spirit that lives in you can quicken your body organs. You need to release the anointing in the name of Jesus Christ. You can say, "Holy Spirit visit my kidney right now, remove all the stones; visit my bladder, and destroy every infirmity."

When you die, all the organs of your body shut down. But the Holy Spirit comes in to your dead body and brings you out of death to life. The Bible says the same spirit that is in you now can fix your womb, can fix your pancreas. Mention the name of Jesus and ask the Holy Spirit bring life to it.

I was praying and the Holy Spirit began to move in me and I was singing a song. I was singing a song in the spirit. The song is, "I know the Spirit that raised Jesus Christ from the dead dwells in me." I was singing it in my spirit and I was sensing a vibration throughout my body.

There is an anointing that you can release into your eyes and you will see clearly. There is an anointing that you can release into your brain, and your memory will be regained. If the Spirit that raised Jesus Christ from the dead dwells in you, He that raised Christ from the dead shall quicken your mortal bodies. The same Spirit is referenced when it says, "Greater is He that is in me than the sickness and afflictions that are in the world." I have the Holy Spirit; the Bible calls Him "the stand by." He stands by you even in the midst of the most difficult situations in order to deliver you. The Holy Spirit doesn't just heal you, He also preserves your health. When the challenges of life come, you need the truth to stand.

Why does God Heal? Because of your office.

1 Peter 2:9: But you are a chosen generation, a royal priesthood, an Holy nation, a peculiar people; That ye should shew forth the praises of Him who hath called you out of darkness into His marvelous light.

The Bible called us priests. But you might think that I am not a priest, that I am a pastor. Being a pastor is different from being a priest. A pastor is a calling. Priesthood is an office. We are all

Priests. The day you were born again, you became the priest of the most high God.

There are requirements for being a priest.

Leviticus 21:18-24: For whatsoever man he be that hath a blemish, he shall not approach: a blind man, or a lame, or he that hath a flat nose, or any thing superfluous,

Or a man that is brokenfooted, or brokenhanded

Or crookbackt, or a dwarf, or that hath a blemish in his eyes, or be scurvy, or scabbed, or hath his stones broken;

No man that hath a blemish of the seed of Aaron the priest shall come nigh to offer the offerings of the LORD made by fire: he hath a blemish; he shall not come nigh to offer the bread of his God. He shall eat the bread if his God, both of the most holy, and of the holy. Only he shall not go in unto the vail, nor come nigh unto the altar, because he hath a blemish; that he profane not my sanctuaries: for I the LORD do sanctify them. And Moses told it unto Aaron, and to his sons, and unto all the children of Israel.

God selected people to be priest. One of the things He does is make sure there are no blemishes in them. When the Bible says you are the priest of the most high God, that means He made provisions to correct whatever is wrong in you.

Original sin brought sickness to this world. Adam and Eve sinned against God and they attracted a plague upon humanity. Jesus Christ came to pay for that sin. Redemption is not complete until the price of your health is paid. The cross of Calvary is the proof that you are not supposed to be sick.

Isaiah 53:1, 4-5: Who hath believed our report? And to whom is the arm of the Lord revealed? ... Surely He hath borne our griefs, and carried our sorrows: yet we did esteem him stricken, smitten of God and afflicted. But He was wounded for our transgressions; He was bruised for our iniquities: the chastisement of our peace was upon him; and with his stripes we are healed.

Those stripes were a price. We will always face one challenge in life or another, but what you know in the days of adversity will determine what you become.

CHAPTER 8

Reigning King

The least of us in the kingdom of God is a winner, a champion, a king. Reigning in life is predicated upon this understanding. By the virtue of redemption by the new birth in Christ Jesus, it is impossible to fail in life. The Lord said it Himself in 1 John 5:4-5: "For whatsoever is born of God overcometh the world: and this is the victory that overcometh the world, even our faith.

> ⁵ Who is he that overcometh the world, but he that believeth that Jesus is the Son of God?"

Say to yourself, "I am an overcomer!" If you believe that Jesus is the Son of God, then consider yourself an overcomer of the world.

God gave you restlessness, a sense of agitation, so that whenever things are not working as God has purposed for you, you realize, "This is not me! I'm more than this!" I am telling you now, by the power of the Holy Ghost, whatsoever is needed in your life for you to get to your throne, you are getting it now, in the mighty name of the Lord Jesus Christ. As a believer, you are sent by God; therefore, there is no obstacle strong enough to stand in your way. When you see obstacles as an opportunity, the situation will change to your advantage. God is not the supporter or backer of failure. As a result, it becomes impossible to fail in the kingdom. Every good and perfect gift comes from the Father of life, so if you are failing in any form, it is not of God. You have the right and authority to abolish and evict failure from your life. To abolish the devil's sponsored outcomes from your life, know that by redemption God made you an overcomer. He put a desire in you that makes you restless until you have vanquished the foe.

Take for example, the miracle that occurred at the Red Sea. The sea did not see the Israelites, it saw God.

Psalm 114:1-8: "When Israel went out of Egypt, the house of Jacob from a people of strange language; Judah was his sanctuary, and Israel his dominion. The sea saw it, and fled: Jordan was driven back. The mountains skipped like rams, and the little hills like lambs. What ailed thee, O thou sea, that thou fleddest? thou Jordan, that thou wast driven back? Ye mountains, that ye skipped like rams; and ye little hills, like lambs? Tremble, thou earth, at the presence of the Lord, at the presence of the God of Jacob; Which turned the rock into a standing water, the flint into a fountain of waters."

The Bible says "the sea saw it." Saw what? The presence, the glory of God, and it fled. "The mountains skipped like rams, and the little hills like lambs." There is no problem in your life that will not jump out of the way in the presence of the Lord. The presence of the Lord obliterated all those insurmountable obstacles. They saw the presence of the Lord and trembled. God sent Israel out of Egypt. His presence abided with them all through the journey. God, likewise, sent you out of the world. His presence is with you always. What Israel witnessed with their physical eyes you must see with the eye of faith, found in the word of God that you are an overcomer by the abiding presence of God. God is the one the obstacles and situations are seeing, not you. There is no reason for you to be afraid because the One whom they see can handle them.

A point in case is the story of Gideon. The Angel of The Lord came to Gideon and said, (paraphrasing} "Oh Gideon, the mighty man of valor, the Lord is with you." Gideon was confused and perplexed about the greeting. Gideon thought, "Why is God calling me a mighty man when I am already failing in life? There is no proving of anything mighty in my life." Then He retorted to God, "If it is true that you are God, if it is true that all you promised is true, why am I in a mess?" Now you would expect God to give an explanation. However, He continued his message. Judges 6:11-14: "

And there came an angel of the Lord, and sat under an oak which was in Ophrah, that pertained unto Joash the Abiezrite: and his son Gideon threshed wheat by the winepress, to hide it from the Midianites. And the angel of the Lord appeared unto him, and said unto him, The Lord is with thee, thou mighty man of valor. And Gideon said unto him, Oh my Lord, if the Lord be with us, why then is all this befallen us? and where be all his miracles which our fathers told us of, saying, Did not the Lord bring us up from Egypt? but now the Lord hath forsaken us, and delivered us into the hands of the Midianites. And the Lord looked upon him, and said, Go in this thy might, and thou shalt save Israel from the hand of the Midianites: have not I sent thee?"

When God said to Gideon, "go in this thy might," which might was He referring to? The concluding statement in verse fourteen, "Have I not sent thee?" answers this question. The might of Gideon was God. John 14:12 says, "Verily, verily, I say unto you, he that believeth on me, the works that I do shall he do also, and greater works than this shall he do, because I go unto my father." Jesus Christ is saying, "Where I stopped is where you are supposed to begin."

John 20:21: "Then said Jesus to them again, Peace be unto you: as my Father hath sent me, even so send I you." If He sends you, then it is Him people will see, not you. Unfortunately, many believers allow themselves to be the one seen because they don't believe the One who sent them.

Gideon complained bitterly when God called him and sent him to smite the Midianites. Gideon, practically speaking, said, "God, I am so little; I am the least in my father's family; I don't have academic credentials; I am not well connected." God, practically speaking, replied, "If you had all that, I wouldn't use you because you would be overqualified." If God is not your qualification, then He won't use you. If you depend on your credentials to qualify you for the work of God, then God will never use you. God wants you to stop disqualifying yourself and begin to believe what He says about you. Redemption, everything that Jesus Christ did on the cross of Calvary, was not done for His benefit, but for yours,

You are, according to Romans 5:17, to reign as kings.

There are forces in this earth right now that are trying to keep you from thinking like a ruler.

Ecclesiastes 10:5: There is an evil which I have seen under the sun...

Those who are ruling are acting like slaves.

This type of action comes with not knowing who you are.

This earth is our inheritance and the saving of souls is our responsibility.

Don't let anybody tell you who you are. Look into His Word and you will see what God says about you and believe it.

Kings reign by truth, not by emotions or religion. Revelation 5:9-10: "And they sung a new song, saying, Thou art worthy to take the book, and to open the seals thereof: for thou wast slain, and hast redeemed us to God by thy blood out of every kindred, and tongue, and people, and nation; And hast made us unto our God kings and priests: and we shall reign on the earth."

If you believe it is true that He died, you should believe that it is true that you must reign. Sadly, not every Christian will experience this; only those who have an understanding of Him will. Only those who believe Him and are willing to trust the Word of the King shall reign on the earth.

In Matthew 4:4, the Lord said, "But He answered and said, It is written, Man shall not live by bread alone, but by every word that proceedeth out of the mouth of God." God is not like man that He would lie. God is not experimenting with the life of His people. If God has spoken it, trust it whole heartedly. Order your steps according to the word of God. I am teaching you this because I want the world around you to know that your Redeemer lives! People must come to an understanding that you are not their mate. Nothing about you is cheap, for there is nothing cheap around God. Heaven's street is paved with gold. Is that cheap? If the things around God are not cheap, don't you dare devalue yourself. Even the devil knows your value. It is you who devalue yourself by looking at yourself through your situation and circumstances, by what people around you are saying, by your lack of academic credentials or personal achievement. If the things around God are valuable, His image (you) cannot be worthless.

Reigning in life means taking charge. It means being influential and impactful. It means the evidence of the presence of God in your life. To reign in life, you must understand three things: 1) You are an heir of God; 2) Call out what you want, i.e., once you have discovered what you want in the word of God, then call for it; and, 3) Be bold. Do not be timid or intimidated by anything or anyone.

1. You are an heir of God. Psalms 24:1: "The earth is the Lord's, and the fulness thereof; the world, and they that dwell therein." According to this scripture, as an heir of God, you are the master of the entire estate of earth. Haggai 2:8: "The silver is mine, and the gold is mine, saith the Lord of hosts." Psalms 50:10: "For every beast of the forest is mine, and the cattle upon a thousand hills." Now, if God owns everything, and you are an heir of God (Romans 8:17) then logically, you have every right to the inheritance of the Father. If your father owns the silver, the gold, the earth, and everyone in it, then there is no way you won't be favored.

   There are many children of God who are faithfully serving God in whatever they know to be faithful, but are suffering in one area or another because they don't know their rights. The older brother of the prodigal son told his father that he had served him for a long time and the father never threw a party for him. The father responded, "Son, I don't need to throw a party for you. You throw a party for yourself, for all these things are yours. Your brother took his, the remaining was all yours. Now that he is back, we share out of yours too." If you do not mature in understanding, God will not transfer the inheritance to you.

   Galatians 4:1-2 (amplified): "Now what I mean [when I talk about children and their guardians] is this: as long as the heir is a child, He does not differ at all from a slave even though he is the [future owner and] master of all [the estate]; but he is under [the authority of] guardians and household administrators *or* managers until the date set by his father [when he is of legal age]."

You own all the estate, but without spiritual maturity, you won't access it. In Ecclesiastes 10:16, the Word says, "Woe to thee, O land, when thy king is a child, and thy princes eat in the morning!" The problem here is that the king, the one who should be reigning, is a child, spiritually immature. The king doesn't know what to do or when to do what they should do. Indeed, a woeful condition for a child of God to be in. The scripture has established that you are an heir; however, the inheritance only come through spiritual maturity.

2. Now that you know you are an heir of God, go into the family will, the Bible, and discover what your inheritance is. When you have discovered it, call it out. Don't expect God to simply do it. The Lord Jesus Christ gives a practical demonstration in Matthew 21:2-3: "Saying unto them, Go into the village over against you, and straightway ye shall find an ass tied, and a colt with her: loose them, and bring them unto me. And if any man say ought unto you, ye shall say, The Lord hath need of them; and straightway he will send them."

Christ demonstrated that He knew He had ownership of all things. I am not telling you to go take people stuff under the pretense that you own all things. I am saying to go into the Word, the Bible, locate what God has promised you, and call it out.

Jesus Christ said, in Matthew 21:3, "If any man say ought unto you, ye shall say, The Lord hath need of them..." That need was promised to the Lord by the prophet Isaiah, so He simply called it out. If you do not go into the Book, then you won't get what you want. In the Book are good houses, a good car parked in the garage, a house full of good things.

Whatsoever God has promised you, it is your mouth that ratifies it. If you don't speak, you won't receive. A king with a closed mouth will live a weak life. Do not say, "I am weak." Rather, say, in the face of trying circumstances, even if you don't feel it, according to the word of the Lord, "I am strong." If you are facing financial down turn, stagnation, or nothingness, say, "The Lord shall supply all my needs, according to his riches in glory, by Christ Jesus." Declare the word of the Lord every day. Confess favor over your life every day. Let kingdom language always proceed from your mouth. Therefore, by Jesus Christ the Son of the living God, I call favor for you; I call wealth for you; I call promotion for you; I call increase for you; I call health for you; I call speed for you. Amen.

3. After making the declaration, be bold. Don't allow room for intimidation. One of the attributes of a king is boldness. The Bible says the righteous is as bold as a lion (Proverbs 28:1). There is a king in you that must be obeyed. Be bold to take the step of faith. Fear does not come from God.

The devil will continue to intimidate you with many reasons about why you can't get where God says you are going. Such intimidations come in the form of, "You can't buy that house. It's not possible. How much is your income? You can't buy that car..." Tell the devil, "I don't spend my income, I spend God's." Until you take the bold step of faith, according to God's Word, you won't experience your expected end. "Greater is He who is in you than he in the world." 1John 4:4

Remember that knowledge is strength. One strength that every believer needs to take that bold step is the knowledge that as Jesus is, so are they, right now. 1 John 4:17: "Herein is our love made perfect, that we may have boldness in the day of judgment: because as He is, so are we in this world." The revelation is, you can live this scripture as if you are in heaven right now. You are like Him right now—not that you will become like Him, but you are exactly like Him right now.

Any obstacle that cannot stand against Jesus, cannot stand against you. In Luke 10:19, the Lord said, "Behold, I give unto you power to tread on serpents and scorpions, and over all the power of the enemy: and nothing shall by any means hurt you." This means that you are entirely too much for whatever situation is confronting you.

Everyone has things happen in their lives. Events come and go. We don't celebrate Christmas every day. You are simply going through an event right now and it is about to end as you step into your inheritance with boldness.

Until you are conscious of your birthright, reigning in life is a sheer struggle. The enemy will take advantage of your ignorance to frustrate you. There are some situations in which God will remain silent. He is silent because He expects you to speak. Many times, we talk to God about what is happening. But, God expects us to speak to the situation. If you do not take charge, according the authority God has given you, nothing will be done about it. Two thousand years ago, Jesus Christ completed the work for your inheritance. Now, boldly enter your inheritance!

CHAPTER 9

Why Praise? (Part 1)

This question is one of the most important questions that can ever be asked. In fact, it is so deep, that I can't possibly explain it all in one chapter, so I will break it down in three parts.

The reason many people do not throw themselves into the hand of God and praise Him as if their lives depended on it is because they don't have an adequate understanding of what they are doing. A lack of understanding of Why Praise have led some to think that praise is a form of entertainment for one's self. However, praise is meant for God; even though you may enjoy giving God praise, it's not meant for you, but for God.

As children of God, born-again Christians, we belong to the kingdom of God. The kingdom of God operates on certain principles, sometimes called the "keys of the kingdom." Christians operating without the understanding of these keys find themselves stranded in some aspect of their lives. These kingdom keys grant us access to our inheritance in the kingdom of God.

The gospel of salvation provides access to a new birth and to heaven; however, it does not guarantee that you will live in peace and enjoy life on the earth. The kingdom keys are the principles that give access to your inheritance in Christ Jesus. Therefore, when you have an understanding of the keys of the kingdom, you can open the doors to your inheritance of peace and enjoyment of life in Christ Jesus.

In Mark 4:11, the Lord Jesus said , "And He said unto them, unto you it is given to know the mystery of the kingdom of God: but unto them that are without, all these things are done in parables." The Lord makes it known that the kingdom of God is packaged in secrets; and not knowing the secrets of the kingdom lead you to live a miserable life.

Some people will ask, "Since God can do anything, why isn't He helping me with this or that?" The reason He is not helping is because you are not using the right key. For example, regardless of your level of education, whether you have a PhD or not, you can't use someone else's house key to open your front door thinking it should work because, after all, it's a house key. Even though it's a key in your hand, it's the wrong key. The kingdom of God works on the same concept: the right key opens the right door. If you don't want to be frustrated in your Christian life, you need to know which key to use for which door. Every door has its own key. And Jesus Christ said this key is packaged in mystery.

Proverbs 25:2: "It is the glory of God to conceal a thing: but the honor of kings is to search out a matter." When God conceals it, we kings are to search it out. The secret things belong to the Lord; the things that are revealed belong to us and to our children. (See Deuteronomy 29:29)

The Lord will open your eyes of understanding this month, and whatsoever belongs to you, you will gain access to it, in the mighty name of Jesus. This month, your days of being cheated are over. This month, all mountains before you shall be leveled. This month all obstacles in your way are removed. This month the enemy will be put to an open shame over your life. This month, you will win all the battles and you will reign supreme, in the mighty name of Jesus.

The devil is not a problem to kingdom citizens because the finished work of Jesus Christ on Calvary fixed the devil problem. The problem with the kingdom citizens is ignorance. The Bible says, In Hosea 4:6, "My people are destroyed for lack of knowledge."

One of the keys of the kingdom is praise. Praise is a powerful tool for releasing the beauty that God has deposited in you. The importance of praise is not well understood, and as a result, a lot people skip praise and worship service and miss out on the blessing. Then, Why Praise?

We praise because our sins are forgiven. Psalms 103:1: "Bless the Lord, O my soul: and all that is within me bless his holy name."

Years ago, this revelation brought rejuvenation to my body system. Sickness and disease lost a grip on me because each day when I wake up, I ask my kidneys to praise Him. The Word says, In 103:1, "Everything that is within me, praise the Lord." I ask my heart, "What are you doing?" Do not limit praise to your lips. Your small intestine can praise Him too. Everything within me must praise Him.

Psalm 103:2-5: Bless the Lord, O my soul, and forget not all his benefits: Who forgiveth all thine iniquities; who healeth all thy diseases; Who redeemeth thy life from destruction; who crowneth thee with lovingkindess and tender mercies; Who satisfieth thy mouth with good things; so that thy youth is renewed like the eagles.

God created the heaven and the earth with the intention of moving heaven to earth. He lost His children, however. The earth was a replica of where God lives. A loving father would never build a house worse than his own for his children. There is no way God would have made man in His image and then put him in a ghetto. In fact, God made His children's house exactly like the one in which He was living. This fact is seen in Genesis 1:28 where God gave man His blessing (to be blessed is to be empowered to perform). God didn't just give man the blessing, He also gave him dominion and fruitfulness; He told him to subdue the earth and replenish it and multiply on the earth. The intent was for man to live in affluence, to be god on earth as God is in heaven.

However, man sinned by eating the fruit of the tree of knowledge of good and evil, a fruit which God had commanded him not to eat. He warned man that on the day he ate it, he would surely die.

God would have been unjust to pardon man for his sin, so He sent them out of the Garden of Eden. It was out of love that He sent them out of the garden so that they would not live in a sinful nature forever. Sin brought the problems of sickness, disease, affliction, and oppression.

But more than the issue of physical and mental wellness, sin took from man his covering—the glory, his throne, his dominion, his wealth, his image. This resulting condition was not just on Adam and Eve, it was on 'his' generation, the whole of mankind. We see this in Romans 5:12: "Wherefore, as by one man sin entered into the world, and death by sin; and so death passed upon all men, for that all have sinned." By one man, sin entered, and with it death, poverty, disease, and all evil.

Romans 5:13-14: (For until the law sin was in the world: but sin is not imputed when there is no law.) Nevertheless death reigned from Adam to Moses, even over them that had not sinned after the similitude of Adams transgression, who is the figure of him that was to come."

Even if in your judgement you deemed yourself righteous, or you have never committed any wrong doing, by simply being born of a woman into this world, you inherited the sin nature. You contracted the virus of sin by birth, and because of sin, death reigns. Since then, until the coming of Jesus Christ, the destiny of humanity was at stake because of sin which brought with it poverty, affliction, sickness, disease.

Jesus Christ came to pay for the sin of man, to redeem man from his sin nature. When you understand that you are no longer under the curse of sin (that sin nature has been expunged in Christ Jesus), you will no longer be under the curse of sickness and disease and it will become impossible for you to live in poverty and oppression, then God is worthy of Praise. The provision for sin to be put away and for everyone to be returned to our estate is what Jesus Christ came to pay.

The effect of sin over the destiny of humanity is probably well over our comprehension. Sin reduced everyone, the entire of mankind, to nothing, It made kings slaves. It put the host of darkness, the devil, over our head and he ruled with an unrelenting hand. A case in point is found in Matthew 9:1-2: "And He entered into a ship, and passed over, and came into his own city. And, behold, they brought to him a man sick of the palsy, lying on a bed: and Jesus seeing their faith said unto the sick of the palsy; Son be of good cheer, thy sins be forgiven thee."

It was not the sins that this man committed which caused him to contract palsy. It was the sin he inherited from Adam that put him in that condition. That is why Jesus Christ said "thy sins be forgiven thee." Sin had to be dealt with before the man could receive healing. The power of sin is so strong that it pollutes the blood system.

Jesus Christ came solely to forgive us our sins so that we can challenge the devil and tell him he has no right to hold us bound. What Satan, the enemy, is using to rule over mankind is the power of sin. But Jesus Christ paid the price.

1 John 1:8, "If we say that we have no sin, we deceive ourselves, and the truth is not in us." but the blood of Jesus cleanses us from all our sins and our iniquities." This means you are washed clean as if sin had never been.

Think about it. How would you feel if I were to tell you right now that you have no sin? Well, that's exactly what I'm saying. In Christ Jesus, you have no sin, you are not a sinner. You have been justified "just as if sin never been." That's your present identity. That's who you are right now in Christ Jesus. Even if you sinned last week or will sin next week, the blood of Jesus washes it away and you are as white as snow, as long as you confess your sins and repent from them.

With this understanding, begin to praise God. Praise Him that your sins are forgiven. Praise Him that Satan has lost his grip on you. Praise Him because you are sickness free. Praise Him that you are not poor, oppressed, afflicted or defeated in life. Praise Him!

The sacrifice of the Lord Jesus cleanses you as if sin had never been. Colossians 2:13: "And you, being dead in your sins and uncircumcision of your flesh, hath He quickened together with him, having forgiven you all trespasses." You being dead have now been cleansed, forgiven. Glory to God! Satan cannot hold you bound anymore. If there is a chronic, generational sickness that runs in your family, there is a disconnection that occurred when your sins were forgiven; therefore, you are no longer a member of that family. You are a member of the household of God. God has cut you off from the sin of Adam and the sin that you may have received through your family line. He connected you with the new birth, of which Jesus is the captain. If you understand this, your praise rhythm will change. Praise Him for the remission of sin and its power is done. Praise Him, for He has rescued you.

Without sin, there is no punishment. Thankfully, sin has been paid for, so we are not under condemnation.

Revelations 1:5-6: "And from Jesus Christ, who is the faithful witness, and the first begotten of the dead, and the prince of the kings of the earth. Unto him that loved us, and washed us from our sins in his own blood, and hath made us kings and priests [we got a promotion] unto God and his Father; to him be glory and dominion for ever and ever. Amen."

God has forgiven us our sins that we may be kings and priests on earth. As a king, everything worships you. This month, everything from the kingdom of darkness will bow before you. Whatsoever is working against your system will bow. Whatsoever is stopping your greatness will die today. Amen. Praise God for your sins are forgiven, that you now have access to the garden.

People who are ignorant of the reality that their sins are forgiven fail in life. Wake up in the morning declaring, "Oh God, I thank you, my sins are forgiven." You can now walk like Jesus Christ who walked the earth in absolute authority over Satan because He was sinless; and that's what you are right now. So, Praise Him.

Once, a lady came to me crying. I asked her, "What's wrong, what happened to you?" She said, "I've messed up my whole life." She goes on to tell me that a while back she had her womb removed. Now she is engaged to be married but she has not told her fiancé of her inability to bear children and her husband to-be wants children. I didn't know what to say. I witnessed Jesus Christ to her. I told her that we are going to choose the Lord and I believe God can do anything. I told her that we are under grace, not the law. The law will tell you that you caused it, but grace will say I fixed it. I said to her, "If you believe God and put your life in His hands, He will fix it." We prayed a simple prayer, and that was it.

Three months later, she began to show signs of being pregnant. She went to the same doctor who removed her womb. The doctor said it was a fibroid cyst and that it should be removed. She came back to me and we prayed, and as we prayed, the Lord said to me, "It's a good fibroid. It should not be removed." I told the lady not to let anyone tamper with it. The fibroid got bigger and she went back to the hospital; the doctors strongly urged her to get it removed. But I told her to leave it alone.

After six months, it was discovered that the fibroid was actually a baby. I'm talking about grace here. The doctors were perplexed as they knew the lady didn't have a womb. They thought the baby was in the lady's stomach. I told her not to worry about where the baby was in her body. Even if the baby is on top of the nose, let it be there. All we want is a baby.

At nine months, it was time to deliver the baby. The doctor wanted to do a cesarean-section. In Africa, a cesarean-section is a dangerous prospect for any woman. As they had her on the stretcher on the way to the operating room, she said she needed to go to the restroom. Instead, she sneaked out of the hospital and rushed to me. I told her to go back to the hospital and deliver her baby. She was upset with me because she thought I was rude, but I was speaking the Word of the Lord. She went back to the hospital. As she was once again being wheeled to the operating room, she delivered the baby on the stretcher. Her womb had been removed, yet she had a baby.

Grace that will overrule your fault. Receive it now, in the name of Jesus. The grace that will give you what you are not qualified for, receive it in the mighty name of Jesus.

Another reason to Praise God is because you are the righteousness of God in Christ Jesus. If you had a full understanding of the finished work of Christ on Calvary, you would dance before God until He calls you to glory. Every day of your life will be a day of praise.

2 Corinthians 5:21: For He hath made him to be sin for us, who knew no sin; that we might be made the righteousness of God in him.

Righteousness means right standing with God. It means standing before God without any fear or inferiority. It means coming into the presence of God with boldness as if nothing has been wrong with you since you were born. It means boldness to enter the throne of grace. Righteousness is not something you get by your own effort. The Bible says in Isaiah 64:6, "But we are all as an unclean thing, and all our righteousness are as filthy rags; and we all do fade as a leaf; and our iniquities, like the wind, have taken us away." The righteousness of the most righteous person, before God, is like filthy rags.

God put righteousness into your life as a gift. Righteousness is not right doing; it's right standing. God gave you a right standing before Himself. As far as God is concerned, that is what He wants, so He gave it to you.

Romans 5:17: For if by one man's offense death reigned by one; much more they which receive abundance of grace and of the gift of righteousness shall reign in life by one, Jesus Christ.

If you were to get a gift from someone, wouldn't you say thank you? Say thank you to God in Praise because He gave you the gift of righteousness. It was an exchange: He became sin; you became righteous. Everything that mankind lost in the garden has been restored to us through the righteousness of God in Christ Jesus. Righteousness destroyed condemnation because everything that was written against you has been written in Jesus' account.

For example, Jesus Christ stood before the tomb of Lazarus, who had been dead for four days, and said, "Lazarus come out," and he came out. Jesus had a right standing with God. It was righteousness at work. No fear. No inferiority. Jesus simply stepped up and called Lazarus and he came out.

Jesus was sleeping on a boat in the sea with His disciples and a menacing storm came and almost overturned the boat. His disciples were overwhelmed with fear and they woke him with a question, "Jesus, don't you care if we perish in this storm?" Jesus got up and rebuked the storm and it calmed.

You may say, "That was Jesus. I couldn't do that." I have news for you—what God can do, you can do because you have a right standing with Him, you are right before Him through the righteousness of Jesus Christ. Remember the exchange? He took my place, that I may take His place.

In any storm, all that God expects from you is to speak to it. Say, "Peace be still." You will have the same result that Jesus did. Lift your hand where you are and Praise Him. He has given you the victory. Walk in the victory of Jesus Christ. This is the most important aspect of your Christian faith; know that you are the righteousness of God in Christ Jesus. You are righteous.

People who are conscious of being righteous in Christ Jesus naturally produce righteous deeds. They are a powerful and masterful force against the attack of Satan. The devil may play with your mind to get you to doubt your right standing with God. The way to overcome this trick is to continue to say, "I am the righteousness of God in Christ Jesus. I am righteous."

Colossians 2:10: And ye are complete in him.

Declare the words: I am complete in Him. I am complete in Christ.

Colossians 2:10 (Amplified Version): "And in Him you have been made complete (achieving spiritual stature through Christ), and He is the head over all rule and authority (of every angelic and earthly power)

This means that every created thing bows to you. Why? Because you are complete in Christ.

> Colossians 1:21-22: And you, that were sometime alienated and enemies in your mind by wicked works, yet now hath he reconciled
>
> [22] In the body of his flesh through death, to present you holy and unblameable and unreproveable in his sight.

If God was standing right in front of you right now, He would look at you and say who is this holy person? Jesus Christ presented you to God and His father, a holy person and that's what you are right now. This understanding will cause you to run away from sin, as the consequence of sin is not unrighteousness but the opening of the door for Satan to gain access to your life. The grace of God cannot abound in the continuance of sin. Meddling with sin will most certainly reduce you to nothing; therefore, eschew sin with a passion.

Praise God for your sins are forgiven. You have been separated from the kingdom of darkness and have been translated into the Kingdom of His dear Son, the kingdom of light. You are in that kingdom fully justified, fully righteous before God. Praise Him with this understanding through faith.

CHAPTER 10

Why Praise (Part 2)

When I think about all the things I did in my early years in the ministry, I can't help but Praise God for bringing me the true knowledge of His word. I remember when I didn't have the knowledge about fasting. Fasting was a big deal for believers in my village. We were taught that you had to fast for at least thirty days before God would work through you. I would fast Monday through Friday, and after I broke my fast on Friday, I would not eat anything else until after 6 pm on Sunday. That was oppression. But we didn't know any better. And we wanted to be spiritual.

If you saw us in those days, you would laugh. We were so puffed up with our religious exercises, and that was all they were—religious exercises. Because we didn't understand why we were fasting, the only results we got were hunger pangs. But I was so determined to punish myself with fasting that I took it to another level. When it was time for me to break my fast, I broke it with bitter leaf. Bitter leaf is a vegetable used for preparing the popular bitter leaf soup. It is also known as Onugbu, Shiwaka & Ewuro by the Igbos, Hausas & Yorubas in Nigeria. Bitter leaf has such a bitter taste to it that you could hardly stand to drink it. I thought the more I punished myself, the more God would work through me. I was so wrong, and I praise God every day for bringing me into the truth and knowledge of His Word.

We are going to move on to another mystery of God as revealed in His Word to comprehend the blessings which rightfully belong to us.

But first, let's look at the character of God. In Numbers 23:19, the Bible says, "God is not a man that He should lie; neither the son of man, that He should repent: hath He said, and shall He not do it? Or hath He spoken, and shall He not make it good?" When He speaks, you can rely on what He says without doubt because His words never fail.

2 Peter 1:3: According as his divine power hath given unto us all things that pertain unto life and godliness, through the knowledge of him that hath called us to glory and virtue.

God said He has given unto you all things that pertain to life and godliness. Take a moment to reflect on the seriousness of this promise: "I have all things right now. God said it. I don't have anything to worry about anymore. God can't lie! I have all things now!"

You may have difficulties accepting this reality because you probably have been reading the Bible as a literature book or a history book or a story book. The Bible is the Word of God, and this is the Word that upholds the planet. The God who said, "let there be light" and there was light, is the same God who said He has given you all things that pertain to life and godliness, be it health, finances, children, home, joy, peace, longevity, even academic success. God has given you everything you need for life; however, you must have the truth that God is not a man and cannot lie established in your heart. And, most importantly, you must have the knowledge of God.

The knowledge of God only comes from the Bible, nowhere else. It takes the knowledge of the truth, not information about the truth, to access the provisions of God for your life. Most Christians, though whole-heartedly serving God, are failing in life, not because of the devil, but because they are not operating in the knowledge of God.

Proverbs 24:10: If thou faint in the day of adversity, thy strength is small.

If you fail in the day of adversity, God says your strength is small. In other words, you have limited knowledge. Proverb 24:5 says, "A wise man is strong; yea, a man of knowledge increaseth strength." The knowledge of the truth gives you strength to stand in the day of adversity. Therefore, if you fail or faint, it is because you lack the knowledge of the word of God. The knowledge of the word of God positions you to disgrace the enemy and the forces of darkness and to humiliate situation and circumstances through the knowledge by applying the wisdom of God, also known as the secrets of God.

Being a Christian is not the same thing as being a kingdom citizen. A kingdom citizen is ever conscious of the fact that the King takes care of him or her. A Christian, on the other hand, is trying to figure out how they will make ends meet.

2 Corinthians 2:14: Now thanks be unto God, which always causeth us to triumph in Christ, and maketh manifest the Savior of His knowledge by us in every place.

God always causes you to triumph in Christ Jesus, therefore there is no possibility of failure in your life. The situation you are going through right now is about to expire, in the mighty name of Jesus. The secret of God is also known as the wisdom of God; it reigns anywhere, anytime, and in all places. Applying the wisdom of God to any situation, guarantees victory over the enemy.

Ephesians 3:10: To the intent that now unto the principalities and powers in heavenly places might be known by the church the manifold wisdom of God.

It is by the church that, in this present time, the angelic rulers and powers in the heavenly world will learn the wisdom of God in all its different forms. God did this according to His eternal purpose, which He achieved through Christ Jesus our Lord. The intention of God is to abase Satan and put him under your feet. The intention of God is for you and me to walk through the valley of the shadow of death with no fear of evil; for us to live free of sickness, fear of premature death, free of any form of evil.

God wants to humble this generation by the demonstration of the power and glory of God in the church. You are the church. Your life must reflect the power and glory of God. Praise is part of the wisdom that God uses to humble the kingdom of darkness. God's way of doing things is called God's wisdom. It's far beyond the wisdom of man. Man can never think it up or rationalize it. It's beyond human understanding.

Romans 11:33: O the depth of the riches both of the wisdom and knowledge of God! How unsearchable are his judgments, and his ways past finding out!

The wisdom of God cannot be found in the laboratory or any human machination. You either believe it or you fail. The wisdom of God may look simple but it is the answer.

Praise is a language system of the kingdom of God. Whenever this language is used, by faith, God is committed, on the spot.

The Effect of Praise

Praise is a weapon of spiritual warfare. Kingdom citizens are in a constant battle with the kingdom of darkness, whether are not they are aware of it. In 2 Corinthians 10:3-4, the Bible says, "For though we walk in the flesh, we do not war after the flesh: (For the weapons of our warfare are not carnal, but mighty through God to the pulling down of strong holds;)." In Ephesians 6:12, the Bible says, "For we wrestle not against flesh and blood, but against principalities, against powers, against rulers of the darkness of this world, against spiritual wickedness in high places."

Unprovoked animosity and hatred directed at you is not necessarily a thought function of the individual from whom it is coming. Instead, it is from the forces of darkness and wickedness. One of the ways you can stop the enemy from advancing into your destiny is praise.

Psalms 149:6-9: Let the high praises of God be in their mouth, and a two-edged sword in their hand; To execute vengeance upon the heathen, and punishments upon the people; To bind their kings with chains, and their nobles with fetters of iron; To execute upon them the judgment written: this honor have all his saints. Praise ye the Lord.

Praising God will bring vengeance upon the enemy. Instead of complaining and griping, burst into praise. It doesn't matter the pedigree of the person standing against you, praise is the weapon that will handle anyone or anything. For any attack against your life, there is a "judgment written." However, the judgment is latent, inactive; praise is required to activate, or "execute" the judgment. Some people wait for God to act. But God is waiting for them to cause Him to execute judgment over the forces that are stopping or hindering their destiny.

It may look so simple, but that is the answer: Praise. Psalms 8:1-2 says, "O lord, our Lord, how excellent is thy name in all the earth! Who has set thy glory above the heavens. Out of the mouth of babes and sucklings hast thou ordained strength. Because of thine enemies, that thou mightest still the enemy and the avenger." The easiest way to win in life is through Praise. When you praise, God is committed to stand against the enemy and immobilize him. Each time you engage in praise, heavenly armies are descending.

Praising God is warfare, so engage in it as if you were engaging in something that will save your life. You can pray amiss. But, you can't praise amiss. You can pray a wrong prayer, but you can't praise a wrong praise.

I was once called to pray for a patient in the hospital. When I got to the hospital and saw the patient, I knew that the individual was dying. The eyes had "turned" already. The Pastor who accompanied me looked at me, I looked at him, and we agreed that the patient was gone. As I stood over the patient, a song came to my spirit. I sang the song about five to seven times, and then suddenly, the patient joined us, singing the song. Praise goes to a place that has been locked up and opens it because it involves God.

Praise is a tool for supernatural supply and multiplication.

Psalms 67:5-7 (this is a secret of the kingdom packaged in the Bible for kingdom citizens, not just for church goers): Let the people praise thee, O God; let all the people praise thee. Then shall the earth yield her increase; and God, even our own God, shall bless us. God shall bless; and all the ends of the earth shall fear him.

Here is a way to experience a fearful, unexplainable blessing. God made the earth to naturally multiply whatever is put into it. However, when man fell, the curse undid the Divine blessing on earth. For this reason, many sow but do not receive the abundance they hoped for. But, in this scripture we see that praise will cause the earth to bring an increase by God blessing the earth for your sake. In Christ Jesus, you are called. Since you are called, there is a supernatural provision available to your calling.

CHAPTER 11

Why Praise? (Part 3)

Revelation is a priceless beauty of redemption because it gives insight into what is in the heart of God.

Daniel 2 tells a story about the power of revelation. Nebuchadnezzar, king of Babylon, had a dream. In the dream, he saw a frightening, perplexing, awesome figure. The king wanted to know the meaning of the dream so he summoned the wise men (astrologers and magicians) of his kingdom. He asked them to first tell him what he dreamed and then give him the interpretation of the dream. The king imposed the penalty of death should the wise men not tell him his dream and the interpretation.

Daniel was one of the wise men of Babylon. When the executioners arrived at Daniel's door to carry out the king's order against the "wise men," Daniel requested an audience with the king. Daniel asked the king for time to seek the Lord for an answer to the king's demand. God revealed to Daniel both the king's dream and the interpretation of the dream. When Daniel related to the king his dream, along with the interpretation, king Nebuchadnezzar fell before Daniel and paid him an offering and promoted him to governor over the province of Babylon. Here's a slave who became governor by the power of revelation. This is a practical demonstration of the power of revelation knowledge.

As a redeemed child of God, what you need to take you to the next level is revelation. Revelation is God's way of ruling the planet. God gave me a revelation to share with you the reasons to praise.

Praise is God's secret to bring anybody out of any dungeon because it commits God's integrity. If you want to knock out all aspects of defeat in your life, you must enter, in your heart, into a diligent praise of God. In praise, you are inviting God into your life, and when God shows up, everything that's not submitted to God dies.

Psalms 92:1 says "It is a good thing to give thanks unto the LORD, and to sing praises unto thy name, O Most High". The same scripture is repeated almost word for word in Psalms 147:1, "Praise ye the Lord: for it is good to sing praises unto our God; for it is pleasant; and praise is comely."

Look at 1 Peter 3:13, "And who is he that will harm you, if ye be followers of that which is good." The Bible says it is a good thing to give thanks unto God Most High, then who will harm you? If you are praising God, you are living in a harm free zone. Giving praises to God from your heart terminates all that is standing against you. Commit yourself to the attitude of praise and worship. Praise Him in the morning. Praise Him in the afternoon. Praise Him in the evening. Praise Him always!

Even if you aren't in the habit of inviting God into your regular dealings, through praise, He comes automatically. Psalms 22:3 says "But thou art holy, O thou that inhabitest the praises of Israel." Praise compels God to show up. Divine presence is all you need on this earth to become untouchable. Begin to use scriptural wisdom to live, for the days ahead are evil.

Psalms 114:1-8: When Israel went out of Egypt, the house of Jacob from a people of strange language; Judah was his sanctuary, and Israel his dominion. The sea saw it, and fled: Jordan was driven back. The mountains skipped like rams, and the little hills like lambs. What ailed thee, O thou sea, that thou fleddest? Thou Jordan, that thou wast driven back? Ye mountains, that ye skipped like rams; and ye little hills, like lambs? Tremble, thou earth, at the presence of the Lord, at the presence of the God of Jacob; Which turned the rock into a standing water, the flint into a fountain of waters.

What causes the mountains and the hills to move out of the way? The presence of the Lord. Praise is the first and foremost catalyst of invoking the Presence of the Lord. Praise releases the voice of the Lord for directions and breakthroughs, and displaces every force of opposition. Psalms 29:3-5 says that "The voice of the Lord is upon the waters: the God of glory thundereth: the Lord is upon many waters. The voice of the Lord is powerful; the voice of the Lord is full of majesty. The voice of the Lord breaketh the cedars; yea, the Lord breaketh the cedars of Lebanon." You can cause the voice of the Lord to come into your life by a song of praise. The voice of the Lord will always empower you against anything that is coming against you.

Praise releases wonders into your life, in that through praise, you are acknowledging God for who He is. Praise is a spiritual language. When you praise Him, God supplies the answer to what you have not spoken. According to the voice of the Lord, every arrow sent in your direction, returns to the shooter, in the mighty name of Jesus. Everything that is designed to stagnate you, to immobilize you, to bring you to shame, by the power of the Holy Spirit, they are destroyed today in the name of Jesus.

CHAPTER 12

The Connecting Force (Part 1)

One thing I have found out about God is that there is nothing usual about Him. Everything about God is extreme. Extreme creation, extreme blessing, extreme power, and extreme conception of His Son. So, you should expect extreme blessings, extreme health, etc. When you have an understanding of what the Word says, it takes you to another realm in life.

I know you are a child of God, but are you connected? Do you even know how to be connected? Understanding the ways of God is the foundation for you to make unusual waves on the earth. The ways of God will bring you to another level of making waves on earth. In Psalm 103:7, the Bible says, "He made known His ways unto Moses, His acts unto the children of Israel." Moses began to make waves in Egypt. Pharaoh became a toy in his hand because Moses understood the ways of God.

There is nothing wrong with you; it's what you don't know that's destroying you. That's why you are toiling. You may think it's the devil, but no, it's not the devil. It's because you do not understand the ways of God.

The ways of God in the life of Moses was so powerful, that what was happening in Egypt could not happen to the children of Israel. The Egyptians were dying in the thousands, however nothing happened to the Israelites. The Bible says the land of Egypt was full of darkness for three solid days, but the children of Israel had light in their dwelling places. Moses began to master every situation. He was controlling everything in the land where he was once a slave. It is not your color, your background, your pedigree, or your culture that is your problem. It's what you don't know—the ways of God.

In this chapter, I want to lay a solid foundation because you need to have an understanding of the truth so that you can master your situations. The Bible says, in Psalm 49:20, "A man that is in honor and understandeth not, is like a beast that perish." I'm not saying that you are not born again, but that you may be living in ignorance.

Jacob said, in Genesis 28; 16, "The Lord is in this place and I know not." Jacob heard from God, and Jacob saw the ladder from the earth touching the heavens, and yet he didn't understand, so he left the place and suffered for twenty years. That shall not be your portion.

There are three types of people on earth. The Jews, the Gentiles, and the Church. The Jews are the descendants of Abraham. Abraham made a covenant with God and God told him everyone that came out of his loins will be for Him. God took over the nation of Israel as His own possession. A Gentile is someone who is not a Jew. If you are not a Jew, you are regarded as a Gentile. Gentiles were believed to not be of God. The Church happened when Jesus Christ rose from the dead and He brought the Gentiles to be part of the covenant.

Ephesians 2:11-15: Wherefore remember, that ye being in time past Gentiles in the flesh, who are called Uncircumcision by that which is called the Circumcision in the flesh made by hands; That at that time ye were without Christ, being aliens from the commonwealth of Israel, and strangers from the covenants of promise, having no hope, and without God in the world: But now in Christ Jesus ye who sometimes were far off are made nigh by the blood of Christ. For He is our peace, who hath made both one, and hath broken down the middle wall of partition between us; Having abolished in his flesh the enmity, even the law of commandments contained in ordinances; for to make in himself of twain one new man, so making peace.

One of the things that characterized the Gentiles' position with God was that they were uncircumcised. If a person was uncircumcised, they died like Goliath. They didn't have a defense. When something hit them, it took them out. They didn't have any right to the covenant because of being uncircumcised.

When David killed Goliath, it wasn't because he had been in battle all of his life. David was not a warrior at that time. David killed Goliath based on if he was circumcised or not. Remember, David said, in 1 Samuel 17:26, "Who is this uncircumcised philistine, that he will defy the army of the Living God? Today, I will kill him."

You are blessed spiritually because you are connected to heaven. You are blessed physically because you are healthy. You are blessed financially because cash is there. Wealth and money are two different things. You can have money and not be wealthy, because when we talk about kingdom prosperity, it's beyond cash. Cash is a part of it, but kingdom prosperity is beyond cash. Kingdom prosperity is peace, joy, and the anointing. You are blessed mentally because nothing comes to you without a solution. That's prosperity: body, soul, and spirit.

Because of your position as a Gentile, you don't have a part in the commonwealth of Israel. That wealth was so strong that it affected Abraham. It affected Isaac. It affected Jacob. Their jobs didn't make them wealthy. Abraham raised cattle, and he was rich with gold and silver. Everyone came and paid respect to him.

if you are a Gentile, you are strangers to the covenant, and have no hope without God in the world. Now if a man is without God in the world, he is hopeless—no defense, no power. He is living on his own, and because of that he is vulnerable.

There are good Christians who don't understand covenant. What's the covenant? Covenant is a defined agreement between God and man that licensed anyone in the covenant to have access to everything that God has. That was why when God made a covenant with Abraham, everything that belonged to God was transferred to Abraham's account.

You can't mess with a covenant friend of God; otherwise God will leave His throne and deal with you. A good example is what happened when Abimelech took Abraham's wife to his bed. Remember Abraham's wife Sarah? Even though Abraham was at fault by telling Abimelech that Sarah was his sister, God told Abimelech that if he touched Sarah, He would kill him. Abraham knew nothing about God speaking to Abimelech. It didn't matter that Abraham lied, Abimelech was cursed and everything in his house was cursed. It was the covenant God had with Abraham that was at work here. That is the mighty power of covenant. God will destroy thousands for covenant. He doesn't joke with covenant. No, not at all.

When God was deciding to destroy Sodom and Gomorrah, He said, "Should I do this thing without talking to Abraham?" It's like God Himself felt He couldn't take a step on this planet because He has a covenant with somebody on earth. He is careful to consider what He does so as not to betray the covenant.

Apart from all of this, we saw how God blessed Abraham with gold and silver. Abraham was not rich because he had a job, He was rich because of covenant.

Genesis 14:18-20: And Melchizedek king of Salem brought forth bread and wine: and He was the priest of the most high God. And He blessed him, and said, Blessed be Abram of the most high God, possessor of heaven and earth: And blessed be the most high God, which hath delivered thine enemies into thy hand. And he gave him tithes of all.

Abraham became the possessor of heaven and earth. Nobody was given heaven without the covenant. If you are a believer and you are ignorant of the covenant, you will be cheated. The Bible says in Ephesians 2:12 (paraphrase): "A Gentile is without God in the world." You don't have any hope. Tomorrow looks bleak.

This point is illustrated in what Rahab said: Judges chapter2: And she said unto the men, I know the Lord hath given you the land, and that your terror is fallen upon us, and that all inhabitants of the land faint because of you. For we have heard how the Lord dried up the water of the red sea because of you, when ye came out of Egypt; and what He did unto the two kings of the Amorites, that were on the other side of Jordan, Sihon and Og, whom ye utterly destroyed. A Gentile is an instrument to test how powerful God is. And the Bible says we were once Gentiles.

Ephesians 2:12-13: That at that time ye were without Christ, being aliens from the commonwealth of Israel, and strangers from the covenants [do you now have an understanding of what covenant is?] of promise, having no hope, [everything looks as if it's going to be the end because we don't have the covenant mind] and without God in the world: But now [the story just changed] in Christ Jesus ye who sometimes were far off are made nigh by the blood of Christ.

You were sometimes far off from what? From the covenant of promise. You were far from that protection; you were far from the money:. Now, by the blood of Jesus, you are brought nigh, brought into protection. "Satan hear me now, don't mess with me, otherwise my covenant partner will hit you hard." What makes the church the most powerful institution ever on this planet is the fact that we are in a covenant with God, the maker of heaven and the earth.

One of our major problems is that we are raised as Gentiles, so we don't understand what covenant is all about. Without covenant, there is no agreement. We live in an age that if you want to make a covenant with people you sign papers. That's what you call covenant. There's no spiritual implication in that. If it does not involve blood, it is not a covenant.

In Leviticus 17:11, the Bible says, "The life of every flesh is the blood." So it is impossible to understand God and His plans and build your faith without understanding what covenant is all about. One thing that will help you come to a place whereby your faith is strengthened is when you declare things with authority, because you have covenant understanding. The moment there is blood, you become blood brothers. You cannot do anything against your blood brother, otherwise the covenant will react.

David and Jonathan were in a covenant. Jonathan would do anything to protect David, even against his father's will. Covenant is stronger than the relationship between siblings, because there are blessings and curses that goes with covenant. The moment the covenant is made you are blood brothers, or blood sisters. You have to protect one another. You have to stand up for one another. If you betray that covenant, you will reap a curse on your head.

Many times, in the western world, we think that blood covenant was started by the devil. Don't believe that. Satan stole it. The issue of covenant of blood started with God. The moment man sinned against God, something happened. Man lost his place; he lost his throne; and he was so scared that he couldn't face God. In fact, he lost confidence in God. When he heard God coming, he ran away. He said, in Genesis chapter 3:10 "I heard your footsteps in the garden and I hid myself." His confidence was no longer there.

God Himself cannot come to the fallen man because the position is now different. This man and woman used to be His image and likeness. Now they have taken on another image—the image of a fallen man that looks exactly like the devil.

So, how will God come to man and reassure man that He still loves him? That He can still take care of him, that He can still take him where He is taking him? God had to step in through a covenant. God trained them to know that He still loved them. He called them, killed an innocent animal (a picture of a Lamb of God), and used the skin of this animal to clothe Adam and Eve. Here the word "clothe" can also be a type of "atonement." He covered their nakedness and He used that blood as a mark of connection, a covenant of blood. "We still have something in common. I am still your God; and one day, I will bring you back to me."

The problem is that the blood of animals can't take away sin, it can only cover it. And it can't cover it for long. But it is an indication that God had a plan. It was God that introduced covenant to man, not the devil. God said, in Psalm 89:34 "My covenant will I not break, nor alter the thing that is gone out of my lips." If you don't understand covenant, there is no way your faith can stand.

We have said so many times that the faith of Abraham was strong. Why would his faith not be strong? He was in a covenant. God came to him and said, "Abraham, can I trust you?" Abraham said, "Yes." God said, "Let me prove my love, lets enter into a covenant." Abraham said, "How, God?" Then God said to Abraham, "Circumcise yourself. Give me your blood." And, at ninety years of age, Abraham circumcised himself. Everybody thought Abraham was insane. They said to him, "We thought you were looking for a child." The Bible says the circumcision was the seal of the covenant.

In 1 Kings, Elijah was facing the four-hundred fifty Baal prophets who talked to Satan. Elijah said, "Oh, God of Abraham, Isaac, and Jacob." He invoked the covenant and God stepped in.

The children of Israel were in bondage for four-hundred thirty years, and the Bible says one day they cried unto the Lord and the Lord heard their cry, and He remembered the covenant He made with Abraham, Isaac, and Jacob and He had respect unto them.

God stepped in because somebody invoked the covenant and that covenant was through circumcision by their father Abraham. When I checked the scripture, I discovered that the circumcision was polluted blood because the blood of Abraham had Adam in it. The blood of Abraham had Adam in it yet God respected it. If you crossed any seed of Abraham, you would incur God's wrath on the spot.

The Israelites were in the wilderness for forty years. They were exposed to all manner of viruses, diseases, oppression, and none of them were feeble. Nobody was sick. They lived in the midst of serious cold with no pneumonia, no chest pain. Even in the wilderness, the covenant was still working. The Covenant was working even with polluted blood.

God said that covenant was not perfect, because it has polluted blood in it. So God decided to offer His own blood that is unpolluted. If you understand what I am saying, you will take over this planet. God depended on the blood of Abraham to make a covenant with Israel. He depends on the blood of His son to make a covenant with you. The moment you receive Jesus into your life, you are stepping into a covenant where you can stand and say, "Because of the blood of Jesus, Satan, you are gone!" The Bible calls it the precious blood of Jesus. It sparks something in heaven. God can't look at the blood and not rise.

Zachariah 9:10-12: And I will cut off the chariot from Ephraim, and the horse from Jerusalem, and the battle bow shall be cut off: and He shall speak peace unto the heathen: and his dominion shall be from sea even to sea, and from the river even to the ends of the earth. As for thee also, by the blood of thy covenant I have sent forth thy prisoners out of the pit wherein is no water. Turn you to the strong hold, ye prisoners of hope: even today do I declare that I will render double unto thee. By the blood of Jesus, everyone in any kind of prison of life today, I release you. And God said, by the blood of covenant, I will take you out of every prison.

Hebrews 7:22: By so much was Jesus made a surety [guarantor of the covenant] of a better testament.

He is the surety. When you invoke the covenant by the blood of Jesus, the heaven pays attention—"what are we to do? Because if they fail, then the death of Jesus would have been in vain." You plead the blood of Jesus over your health, over your finances, and God steps in and His Word begins to work. The terms of the covenant are the Book (when I say "Book," I'm talking about the Bible). You go to the Book to find out what the covenant contains. If you don't go to the Book, you don't know what your right is in the covenant.

When I was still residing in Africa, I loved soccer. I still love it, but I don't play it. In those days, I played it. I had a classmate who lived in the city. I lived in the village, so I had never been to a movie house or cinema. We didn't have those in the village. But he lived in the city and commuted to school in the village every day. He would come and tell me about Bruce Lee. I had never heard of Bruce Lee, but this guy told all kinds of stories about Bruce Lee. He told how Bruce Lee made moves like a snake, He would strike you, and it would be like a bite. Then he told me that when Bruce Lee wanted to go to another level, and he was very angry, he would make a certain move and take a pound of flesh from your body when he hit you.

I was afraid because the guy said that Bruce Lee trained him and taught him all those deadly moves. Can you see what happened here? This guy planted fear in my heart. This guy was a real bully. We had to share a bench in our classroom, but many times the guy would take over half of my side of the bench, and if I protested, he would make one of those moves and I let him have as much of the bench as he wanted. He took my pens, my food, my money. This guy was really bullying me.

One day, we were playing soccer. I was already on the field playing when he arrived. In those days, they called it sets. You had to wait your turn. It was my turn and the guy saw me in line, and he said, "Go and sit down. You are not playing. I am going to take you turn." Since I was afraid of him, I started to go sit down, but then the other students began to pick at me for being scared. And

I thought, "I really want to play, and I can't let this guy continue to bully me. Everyone is laughing at me."

Before I knew what I was doing, the guy rushed me. I don't know if it was one clean slap or what, but I know I saw stars. He slapped me and said, "Go and sit down!" The other students went wild and began to shout and pick at me even more. I decided, "If you are going to kill me, kill me now. You have been Bruce Lee-ing me all these days." I rushed him. I was surprised at how light he was. I picked him up like paper and slammed him to the ground. I shouted at him, "You are the one who is not playing." And from that day, he never bothered me again. In fact, he came to me and wanted us to be friends.

When you know covenant, you connect with strength that you have that you have not used. Most of the things that are shouting against you are there because you don't know you are in a covenant. Ezekiel chapter 34: "I will cause that evil beast to cease out of your land and you shall dwell safely in the land."

Communion is a way to reenter into the covenant. I was in New York a few years ago, preaching. When I finished preaching, a Pastor and his wife whom I met at the service invited me to their house to have dinner. . The wife sat at the dinner table in her house with a bottle of water and said, "Bishop, we have been going through so much." I said, "What is going on?"

She told me about having heart surgery and that there were complications from it that made it so painful. She said the situation had brought so many things to their marriage. I looked at the woman, and asked, "Are you saved?" She nodded. I said, "We can give you a brand new heart right now." She said with surprise, "A brand new heart?" The husband looked at me with doubt on his face.

The Lord told me to share communion with them. I asked them if they had communion. The husband answered no. I asked, "Do you have crackers and soda?" He said yes. We put the crackers and soda on the table and I blessed them and served them. As I finished serving, I prayed, "Father we thank you."

I had not prayed two minutes before I saw Jesus Christ come into the house and He gave this woman a brand new heart. I told her, "In the next three days, go back to the hospital and find out what is going on with your heart. God told me you have a brand-new heart."

She went to the hospital and they discovered that the pacemaker was no longer there. The doctors who installed it were confused. It was a brand-new heart. Her husband travelled to Africa to come and meet with me. He said, "This is so strange." I told him that it is normal with this God. There is nothing too hard for God. Invoke the covenant and God will step into your situation every time.

CHAPTER 13

The Connecting Force (Part 2)

In the last chapter, I shared some important points about covenant, and I want you to know that, until you truly understand covenant, you can't walk with God. You can't enjoy Him and your faith can never grow because covenant is the basis of our relationship with God. God is too high, too big, too strong and too awesome. Without covenant He can't deal with mere man. Covenant brings God to the level of man, and brings man to the level of Almighty God. Therefore, you can't live in the supernatural without an understanding of what covenant is all about. Everything about God is based on covenant. It takes the burden from you and puts it on Him. And it is only Him who can never feel pressure from that burden. Covenant gives you a direct link with who He is and helps you enjoy the supernatural power that made the heaven and earth to stand where it is today.

It was the covenant of Jehovah that exempted Abraham from the pressure of the world and all the things he went through when he was here. He was living strange in the midst of the wicked world. During his time, it looked like Abraham was invisible to the forces of Satan. The pressure of the world did not have any effect over him. His faith grew daily, because he knew God was with him.

Who will stand against the God of the heaven and the earth and remain standing? His glory alone will melt you. He was in the midst of the Israelites and the Egyptians. God was a pillar of cloud, and the cloud was so thick that they couldn't penetrate it.

And in the night, He was a pillar of fire, and if you didn't want to be burned into ashes, then you didn't go into it. God was there because of covenant. There are too many Christians, covenant people, who are dying unnecessarily. The Bible says in Psalms 82:5, "they know not, nor will they understand..." Without God in the world, you are hopeless. Without God in the world, you are open to attack. Without God in the world, you live a life of mockery. The Bible says you have no hope, no God, you are a stranger to the covenant of promise. But when you come to God through the blood of Jesus Christ, all the blessings of the covenant come into your life. You are connected by the blood of Christ.

Abraham's story changed because of the covenant connection. What happened in the life of Abraham was something that only God can do. God came to him when Abraham was seventy-five years old. His wife was sixty-five.

The covenant that God made with Abraham was the covenant of circumcision. Some of us do not know, when God asked Abraham to bring his son, why Abraham did not say no. He did not say no because they had a covenant relationship, and it was a covenant of blood.

The covenant is expressed in words in Psalms 89:34: "My covenant will I not break, nor alter the thing that is gone out of my lips."

"I will not break this covenant. And this covenant is my word." Each time you agree with the word of the covenant, something immediately starts happening in your life independent of what you know. God is working something beyond your strength. When He said in Psalms 105:8, "He hath remembered His covenant forever, the word which He commanded to a thousand generations," covenant is expressed in words. This is the only way you can know your portion of the covenant. The covenant is already made, and God wants you to know what belongs to you in the covenant. It is not what you struggle to get.

If you rent an apartment, the first thing they want you to do is to sign a lease. The moment you sign that lease, you are in a contract. Most people would think that the contract becomes a covenant between you and the company or landlord. But that is not a covenant because no blood is involved. You can go back and say, "I don't want this apartment anymore," and you will pay a monetary penalty. With covenant, you pay the penalty with your life. That's why no one wants to break covenant.

Let's look at it from another angle. It was the word *covenant* that gave victory to the children of Israel, and destroyed the Ammonites and the Moabites the day they met at Mount Sinai.

2 Chronicles 20:1-25: Verses 1-2: It came to pass after this also, that the children of Moab, and the children of Ammon, and with them other beside the Ammonites, came against Jehoshaphat to battle. Then there came some that told Jehoshaphat, saying, There cometh a great multitude against thee from beyond the sea on this side Syria; and, behold, they be in Hazazontamar, which is Engedi. [The days of being pushed around by the forces of darkness is over right now. Can you imagine them telling Jehoshaphat, there are people surrounding this place to kill everybody here. They weren't prepared for war, there was no announcement. I don't know whether you've been there; you don't expect this, it's not something you have been praying about, something different is in your plan and suddenly something showed up that puts your life in danger.]

Verse 3: And Jehoshaphat feared, and set himself to seek the LORD, and proclaimed a fast throughout all Judah. [Instead of crying, Jehoshaphat sought the face of the Lord. Why? Because there was something that this man knew about God and keeping covenant.]

Verse 4: And Judah gathered themselves together, to ask help of the LORD: even out of all the cities of Judah they came to seek the LORD. [The first thing Jehoshaphat did was to pull the string of the covenant. "Oh God of our fathers…" When you get to a place where it looks as if things are collapsing, pull the string of the covenant. If you can get hold of the word of the covenant, God is committed.]

Verse 5-7: And Jehoshaphat stood in the congregation of Judah and Jerusalem, in the house of the LORD before the new court, and said, O LORD God of our fathers, art not thou God in heaven? And rulest not thou over all the kingdoms of the heathen? And in thine hand is there not power and might, so that none is able to withstand thee? Art not thou our God, who didst drive out the inhabitants of this land before thy people Israel, and gavest it to the seed of Abraham thy friend for ever? [They were pulling the string. If you read Genesis 13:14-15, you discover that God told Abraham, just get out there, count the stars and so shall thy seed be. And He said, "Unto that place you have seen, northward, eastward, unto you will I give it and unto thy seed after thee." Jehoshaphat was not sitting looking for somebody to come and pity him. You too could pray in the same manner Jehoshaphat prayed by invoking the term of the covenant. For example, " Art thou not the God in heaven that said by the stripes of Jesus I've been healed? Art thou not God in heaven? Do not consider what happened to other people who had the illness you have. Do not think to yourself, if I die, I will be with Jesus. Refused to die prematurely. Refuse to be killed by the enemy! I Decide to sleep. There are people who are killed, and there are people who fall asleep. In church you don't die, you sleep, because you only sleep when you have finished your assignment. But in the midst of your assignment, if you die, the enemy have killed you.]

Verse 8-11: And they dwelt therein, and have built thee a sanctuary therein for thy name, saying, if, when evil cometh upon us, as the sword, judgment, or pestilence, or famine, we stand before this house, and in thy presence, (for thy name is in this house) and cry unto thee in our affliction, then thou wilt hear and help. And now, behold, the children of Ammon and Moab and mount Seir, whom thou wouldest not let Israel invade, when they came out of the land of Egypt, but they turned from them, and destroyed them not; Behold, I say, how they reward us, to come to cast us out of thy possession, which thou hast given us to inherit.

Verse 12-13: O our God, wilt thou not judge them? For we have no might against this great company that cometh against us; neither know we what to do: but our eyes are upon thee. And all Judah stood before the LORD, with their little ones, their wives, and their children. [We saw the way everybody began to talk to God, and God heard.]

Verse 14-15: Then upon Jahaziel the son of Zechariah, the son of Benaiah, the son of Jeiel, the son of Mattaniah, a Levite of the sons of Asaph, came the Spirit of the LORD in the midst of the congregation; and he said, Hearken ye, all Judah, and ye inhabitants of Jerusalem, and thou king Jehoshaphat., thus saith the LORD unto you, Be not afraid nor dismayed by reason of this great multitude; for the battle is not yours, but God's. [You pull the string—this battle is not yours but God's. Each time you invoke the covenant, God can't keep quiet.]

Verse 16-18: Tomorrow go ye down against them: behold, they come up by the cliff of Ziz; and ye shall find them at the end of the brook, before the wilderness of Jeruel. Ye shall not need to fight in this battle: set yourselves, stand ye still, and see the salvation of the LORD with you, O Judah and Jerusalem: fear not, nor be dismayed; tomorrow go out against them: for the LORD will be with you. And Jehoshaphat bowed his head with his face to the ground. [They started the praise before the battle started. Do you know why? They heard a word of the covenant. Each time you hear a word of the covenant, you don't go back home looking as if things never changed. You dance from church to your house. That is what makes the covenant work. Many times when you look at what you see physically, nothing changes. Now they came in. I'm talking about somebody that did not know whether tomorrow will still meet him on the surface of the earth. The Bible says the multitude of the Ammonites, Moabites, and the people of Mount Seir surrounded the nation of Israel. And this man heard a word of the covenant, "You don't need to fight." They have never seen God step down to fight but they know when He speaks, He backs His words, and they began to praise Him.]

Verse 22: And when they began to sing and to praise, the LORD set ambushments against the children of Ammon, Moab, and Mouth Seir, which were come against Judah; and they were smitten. [And when they began to sing, they didn't just start singing. This is where the church has a lot of problems. You hear nothing from God; there's no scripture that you are meditating on. There's no scripture that's coming to your spirit. Praise becomes a burden. Everyone is doing like this…(dancing around the church). You're saying are they stupid?… The person dancing with style heard something you didn't hear. That's why people come to church, other people are dancing and you look at them and say,. "As depressed as I am, you are dancing?" Because you are depressed is why you can't dance. You hear nothing. If you hear the word of the covenant, you will dance because you know the moment He speaks, He is committed. When the Israelites began to sing and to praise, the Lord set ambushes. Remember, God just told them come and watch, you won't need to fight in this. They went to battle with choirs, dancing as if they are strange. And God set ambushment for the children of Ammon.] See verse 23 For the children of Ammon and Moab stood up against the inhabitants of mount Seir, utterly to slay and destroy them: and when they had made an end of the inhabitants of Seir, every one helped to destroy another. [When you hear a word like this, you know when I speak it that it's not my word, it came by the spirit, and you dance to it. People that you didn't know look at you and say, "He is too much." Let it be too much of you so that you will be too much for them.]

Verse 24: And when Judah came toward the watch tower in the wilderness, they looked unto the multitude, and behold, they were dead bodies fallen to the earth, and none escaped. . "And behold their dead bodies fallen to the earth, and none escaped," and there were no more to contest with them.

Verse 25: And when Jehoshaphat and his people came to take away the spoil of them, they found among them in abundance both riches with the dead bodies, and precious jewels, which they stripped off for themselves, more than they could carry away; and they were three days in gathering of the spoil, it was so much.

The spoil was too much. The God of covenant went ahead of them. The Scripture says God turned them against themselves. Jehoshaphat didn't start his prayer by begging. The whole scenario started by pulling the string of the covenant. If Jehoshaphat knew nothing about the covenant, they would be saying, "Oh God, they are killing us." They would be crying and nothing would happen to save them.

The new covenant that superseded the one they provoked that day was made by the precious blood of Jesus. The covenant that God had as a covenant with Abraham was with polluted blood. Do you remember that? Why do I say that? Because Abraham came out of Adam. Jesus came out of God. The Bible says, in 1Peter 1:19 "But with the precious blood of Christ, as of a lamb without blemish and without spot." He has pure blood that has no link with the blood of Adam in the Garden of Eden. That is why the Bible says in Hebrews, This blood is with a better promise.

Thank God for the blessing. Thank God for the promises that came through the covenant of Abraham. We are talking about a new covenant with better promises, and that's why the Bible says the blood of Jesus is not just for our atonement. The blood is for the remission of sin. Remission means to take out, to purge out, or to purge it. It doesn't cover our sin; it purges it and takes it out completely. If you don't have sin inside of you, Satan doesn't have anything to lay his hand on to punish you. It's nothing that you have done. It is a covenant with God. "If you shed the blood, anyone that believes in you, their sins will be taken out immediately." When you see a scripture that says, "The blood of Jesus cleanses us from all our sins and our iniquities," all you need to do is to repent of your sin and begin to give Him thanks.

That was what the Israelites did. The moment they heard the word of the covenant, they began to dance. They repented. They were dancing and jumping. It looked crazy because nothing positive had happened yet. But they knew the covenant is standing.

This same covenant that God had with Jesus that connected you and me by redemption took our sicknesses and our diseases. All you need to do is to go and locate the covenant, pull the string of the covenant, believe it, and thank Him for it.

The reason a lot of people don't have testimonies is because there are too many lazy people in church. It starts with complaining about the services going too late. But they must know that you don't get the best out of God by doing drive thru church, or microwave versions of church services. That is why, little by little, the church looks like we are always in a hurry. Gradually, sickness takes over, poverty takes over, and demonic forces take over. When we are supposed to talk, we don't know what to say because we don't hear the word of the covenant anymore. We want to hear what we want to hear so that we can quickly rush out. People today are looking more for excitement than they are for changed lives. As long as the speaker is exciting, then you think it was a great service. But if you can't look at your life and see it changing and conforming to the word of God, then excitement means nothing.

You don't need to be poor; the covenant took care of that. You belong to the commonwealth of Israel. The Bible says you are a peculiar people. Peculiar! To be peculiar means to be outstanding, to be different, and to be special. Not because of who you are or what you have done, but because it is in the covenant package that God has with Jesus. You and I were not there, but there was a covenant made between God and Jesus that involves us. In 1 Peter 2:9-10, the Bible says, "We are a royal priesthood, a holy nation, and a peculiar people. He has called us out of darkness into His marvelous light. Which in time past were not a people but are now the people of God. We have not obtained mercy but now mercy is our name. We have obtained the Mercy of God."

When Jesus Christ came to earth, He said in John 8:29 : "And he that sent me is with me: the Father hath not left me alone; for I do always those things that please him." He made a covenant with Him.

Hebrews 7:25: Wherefore He is able also to save them to the uttermost that come unto God by him, seeing He ever liveth to make intercession for them.

That scripture is a covenant word. God remembers what He said to Jesus. Jesus' intercession takes over, and everything you ask comes to your table. If you believe in the covenant of the blood of Jesus, each time you plead the blood or you engage in communion, you are ratifying the fact that this covenant is real. I'm part of this covenant. I'm at the same table with The Father, Son, and Holy Spirit. The same thing that is happening in heaven must repeat itself in my life. That's all. It's not a church ritual.

Now, if covenant fails, then God is no longer the God of the universe. There are times that God, because of what we have done, wants to punish us, but covenant won't allow it. I'm telling you the truth. I can take you through the scripture, in Exodus 32; there was a time that the children of Israel sinned against The Lord. They complained and God was so angry, that God came to Moses and said "Moses, clear off, clear off, let me destroy this people."

God said He would destroy the people and then raise up another people, a new generation. But when Moses heard that, he said, "God, I heard what you said, and I don't agree. If you destroy these people because of what they did to make you angry, what are you going to tell Abraham, Isaac, and Jacob? Remember you made a covenant with them, not with me." It was covenant that kept God from destroying the people.

Raise your right hand and say these words: "I am in a covenant by the blood of Jesus, therefore, let no man trouble me. I have on my body the mark of Christ. I am the righteousness of God in Christ Jesus. By covenant, the One that made the heaven and the earth is with me right now. Therefore, as mountains are round about Jerusalem, God is with me right now and forever. I'm a believer. I'm a child of God, therefore, I overcome the world and every satanic force, because greater is He that is in me, than he that is in the world. No evil, no sorrow, no affliction, no poverty, no disease, no sickness, will come to my dwelling place in the name of Jesus. My destiny is marked with the blood of Jesus. Thank you, Father; I praise you for the word of the covenant, In Jesus name."

www.ingramcontent.com/pod-product-compliance
Lightning Source LLC
Chambersburg PA
CBHW052157110526
44591CB00012B/1981